WHEN GOD
SPEAKS

Books by Joshua Giles

Prophetic Forecast
Mantled for Greatness
Prophetic Reset
When God Speaks

WHEN GOD SPEAKS

Thrive in Uncertain Times and Gain Confidence for Your Future

JOSHUA GILES

Chosen

a division of Baker Publishing Group
Minneapolis, Minnesota

Published by Chosen Books
Minneapolis, Minnesota
ChosenBooks.com

Chosen Books is a division of
Baker Publishing Group, Grand Rapids, Michigan

Printed in the United States of America

Library of Congress Cataloging-in-Publication Data

Names: Giles, Joshua, author.
Title: When God speaks : thrive in uncertain times and gain confidence for your future / Joshua Giles.
Description: Minneapolis, Minnesota : Chosen Books, a division of Baker Publishing Group, [2025] | Includes
    bibliographical references.
Identifiers: LCCN 2024031342 | ISBN 9780800772529 (cloth) | ISBN 9780800773311 (paper) | ISBN 9781493448821
    (ebook)
Subjects: LCSH: Bible. Prophesies. | Christian life.
Classification: LCC BS647.3 .G65 2025 | DDC 220.1/5—dc23/eng/20241009
LC record available at https://lccn.loc.gov/2024031342

Cover design by Peter Gloege, Look Design Studio.

The Author is represented by the literary agency of Embolden Media Group.

Baker Publishing Group publications use paper produced from sustainable forestry practices and postconsumer waste whenever possible.

25 26 27 28 29 30 31   7 6 5 4 3 2

Contents

PART ONE

UNDERSTANDING YOUR PROPHETIC NATURE

1

You Carry the Future

God has made everything beautiful for its own time. He has planted
eternity in the human heart . . .

Ecclesiastes 3:11 NLT

The wheels hit the pavement at full force, making a shrill, high-pitched,
screeching sound—the sound of thousands of pounds of metal colliding
with rubber and asphalt. The plane had landed in Tel Aviv, Israel. I was
excited and nervous, and I didn't know what to expect. This was only the
second international trip I had ever been on. My feet touched the ground,
and surprisingly, it felt like being in a familiar place. Yet I had never been
there. I couldn't quite pinpoint the feeling, until the gate agent on the jet
bridge shouted, "*Welcome home!*"

Though I was a bit disoriented from the twelve-hour flight, I pushed
through the jet lag and thought to myself, *Ahh, it feels like home!* This
would be the beginning of a years-long relationship with traveling to Israel,
ministering to government leaders, helping Ethiopian Jews, bringing over
group tours, and ministering to groups of people there.

I was soon greeted by my host, Shlomo. He was loud, had a heavy accent,
and was very informative about the area. He knew absolutely everyone and

everything you needed to know about the geography, topography, and history of Israel. He was the exact person I needed to host me. The journey started. I met some of the most amazing people, saw all the major biblical sites, and completed a ministry assignment. It was exhilarating! If it was at all possible to fall in love with a country, I did.

Soon after I returned to the States, I was given an assignment to go back to Israel. I had been expectantly awaiting this trip, because the Lord had given me the word that it would be a divinely orchestrated encounter. While in Israel this time around, I was contacted by a man who was on fire for God. He was the kind of person who had so much electrifying energy and excitement coming through him that when you talked to him, you could almost feel the hairs on your arms standing up. I had met him about seven years earlier, when he was living in the United States. He was an invited guest at a conference my church was hosting. At that time, I didn't have a forefront ministry, I wasn't a pastor, and nobody really knew who I was. I was flowing in prophetic ministry and singing on the worship team. Honestly, in those years I would fill in wherever there was a need in the church.

It just so happened that at this service where I first met him, I was ushering, standing at the side door of the meeting space. In the middle of the service, the person presiding somehow felt led to call me up to exhort the people. I didn't really like being in front of a crowd, although at times I had to be. I hesitantly started walking to the front, saying to myself, *I don't have a word or anything to say. Why are they calling me up here?*

I laugh at it now, but it was totally God. I had this completely empty feeling on my way up front. I was trying to think of something to say and came up with nothing. Of course, the walk felt like an eternity. I finally made it and reached for the microphone. As soon as my hand touched the mic, the word of the Lord jumped in my spirit. It felt like gallons of water flooding my being. It was kind of an out-of-body experience. I seemed to be on autopilot as the Holy Spirit began to speak through me.

I stood directly in front of this invited guest and began to prophesy to him. The word of the Lord came that this man of God would move to Israel, and by the time he got there, war would be brewing. I said that the Lord told me this man would be called in like a general. He would be working with a paramilitary unit. In the Spirit, he was a general. I then heard the Lord say something to me that I had rarely heard before. In a vision, I saw millions of dollars being given to this man, and I heard the Lord say that soon he would be given a massive amount of money. God told me to tell him that he would purchase a property in Israel that would become a base for him.

The anointing was so strong in the room that the guest jumped up on his feet, yelling "*Prophesy!*" He continued with shouts of "*Hallelujah! Hallelujah!*" After the service, he found me and asked me to write the prophetic word down for him. There were more details to it that are too personal to record here, but I did as he asked. I wrote the words down, gave them to him, and that was it.

Pretty soon, this occurrence faded to the back of my mind. Years passed, and I had almost completely forgotten about it. Fast-forward to this significant Israel trip. I ended up crossing paths with this same man. I met him in Tel Aviv after not having seen him for seven years. He still had that same electrifying energy, that same deep belly laughter, and he was still so on fire for the Holy Spirit. He told me, "Joshua, I've carried the word you gave me in my Bible for seven years." He looked at me with blazing eyes and added, "You don't know, do you? Everything you spoke in your prophetic word came to pass. It was just a few short months after the word you gave that I received the largest wire transfer I've ever seen in my life."

By this time, his face was beaming, and his voice was escalating. He continued, "When you gave me that word, I was in the process of moving my family and myself to Israel. I had no more money and had a leader in my church in the United States who walked away with half the members. I was experiencing a lot of attacks."

I could tell he was reliving the events as he shared them. He said, "Joshua, it was just a short time after that when I received millions of dollars, just as you prophesied. But get this—it was from an anonymous donor." Then he shouted, "I still don't know *who* the person is!"

He was able to purchase that property in Israel. It was such a massive purchase that it made the Forbes list. Only God could do something like that. Over the years, this man became one of my closest friends and covenant brothers. I'll never forget what he said to me that day. He had no idea how secretly discouraged I was in ministry. He had no idea that I didn't really desire to prophesy in that way. I had experienced attacks, criticism, and backlash from people I knew. He looked me in the eyes and said with a deep, stern, yet loving voice, "Don't you *ever* stop prophesying!"

The Future Is in Your DNA

You see, I was carrying the future, and I didn't know it. All those years before, when I had prophesied to this man, not knowing his situation, I hadn't realized that the future was in me. When I gave him those extraordinary prophetic words, I was broke. I mean, my bank account was negative. Not only did I not have money, but I also felt stuck in a poverty cycle and had no clue how to start fully moving in my purpose. But the Lord spoke to me at that exact moment when the man uttered those words "Don't you *ever* stop prophesying!" God said to me, *See, Joshua, you had future millions in you, but you didn't know it.*

That man's economy and personal life shifted because of the words God placed in my mouth for him. It's important to note that you carry the future in words, ideas, and thoughts. It's literally living on the inside of you. When this series of events occurred, I was just beginning to understand this concept. The Holy Spirit would soon teach me that He has equipped us and given us everything we will have in the future—it's on the inside of us. Even if your condition or situation looks bleak right now, you already are what you will be. You already possess what you will have. Every believer can hear from God and share that encouraging message with someone else. This doesn't mean all believers are prophets or will have a public speaking or platform ministry. Yet God can use any of us to release a prophetic word. He has to plant a word you release in your spirit first, of course. This means that before you share a word with someone else, you already have it in you.

Right now, in this very moment, the future is coursing through your veins. You just need to realize it. In Scripture, Jacob had an encounter with God that changed his life forever. Genesis 28:10–12 (esv) describes it:

> Jacob left Beersheba and went toward Haran. And he came to a certain
> place and stayed there that night, because the sun had set. Taking one of the

stones of the place, he put it under his head and lay down in that place to sleep. And he dreamed, and behold, there was a ladder set up on the earth, and the top of it reached to heaven. And behold, the angels of God were ascending and descending on it!

Jacob had stopped to rest in what he thought was just a random place. As he went to sleep, the Lord showed him a glimpse of what was happening in the realm of the spirit. He saw a ladder going from earth to heaven in that place. The angels were ascending and descending on it. Wow, this was a divine portal he saw that had opened up, connecting the natural world to the eternal world. Clearly, these messenger angels were bringing something from one world to the other. It is believed that angels may at times come to get our words, prayers, and the praise we release to the heavenly Father. This is seen in Daniel 10:12 (KJV), when an angel who visited Daniel told him, "I am come for thy words." I believe that they bring our prayers and words up to God and then bring down answers and even supernatural resources to us.

Jacob realized that what he saw was special. God was revealing a hidden truth to him. Genesis 28:16–17 says, "Then Jacob awoke from his sleep and said, 'Surely the LORD is in this place, and I did not know it.' And he was afraid and said, 'How awesome is this place! This is none other than the house of God, and this is the gate of heaven.'" He had found the very access point from the natural world into the spiritual world. He had stumbled upon the house of God and the gate to where God lives.

Jacob's powerful encounter shows us a vivid image of what God has placed on the inside of every person, especially those who would give their hearts to Him. Ecclesiastes 3:11 reveals, "He has made everything beautiful in its time. Also He has put eternity in their hearts." Some translations say He has placed the "world" in the hearts of mankind. The words are translated differently because the editors were trying to find the most accurate word to describe what God has placed in our hearts. The word there in Hebrew is *ôwlâm*, and it can be defined as eternity and the future.[1] That's right—God has placed the future in your heart!

Why is this so important? Because the heart pumps blood throughout the entire body. Ecclesiastes 3:11 is showing us a mystery. God placed the future in human DNA. Deoxyribonucleic acid (DNA) is made up of two linked strands that wind around each other, known as a double helix. It resembles a twisted ladder. Ribonucleic acid (RNA) is a messenger that carries instructions from the DNA. RNA carries genetic information up and down the double helix (ladder). Does this sound familiar? It's the exact replica of Jacob's night vision of a ladder. He saw angels—messengers—going up and down the ladder from earth to heaven. I see Jacob's ladder as symbolic of human DNA. The angels are symbolic of the RNA messengers carrying information. This means that the house of God is within you. The gate of God is within you. Eternity is within you. The future is within you!

In 1 Corinthians 6:19, the apostle Paul says it this way: "Do you not know that your body is the temple of the Holy Spirit who is in you, whom you have from God, and you are not your own?" God living in you takes on a whole new meaning when you realize that He has placed Himself within your DNA.

Unlocking Your Prophetic Future

I believe that God wants to partner with you to empower you to see and co-create the future He has planned for your life. When you realize that God has given you the ability to capture the future ahead of time, through the grace and power of Jesus Christ working inside you, then you will be confident in His plans for your life. You don't have to think about the future with anxiety. God is the designer of our future and wants us to be aware of His major plans for what's coming.

What do I mean by capturing the future He has planned? Here are some ways that you can embrace and unlock God's amazing future for your life and experience it in the now: *calling those things that are not as though they are*, *releasing eternity into time through prayer*, and *activating your prophetic promise*. Let's look at each of these ways a little more closely.

Calling those things that are not as though they are

In Romans 4:17, Paul uses Abraham as an example to show that because Abraham believed, he was able to obtain the promise. It is through faith that we receive salvation. It is through faith that we are made righteous through Christ. The verse says, "As it is written: 'I have made you a father of many nations.' He [Abraham] is our father in the sight of God, in whom he believed—the God who gives life to the dead and calls into being things that were not" (NIV). The New Living Translation says God "creates new things out of nothing." It is through faith that we are able to unlock the creative power of God and walk in purpose. God calls things forth into our now that we cannot see. We then have the ability to speak what God has said. That is prophecy. It's speaking the things that do not exist yet into being.

Releasing eternity into time through prayer

As I mentioned earlier, eternity is coursing through your veins. That includes God's future plans for you. The gate of God is within you. Jesus put it this way in Luke 17:21 (KJV): "Behold, the kingdom is within you." This means that God's abode is not some earthly external edifice or physical structure. His powerful, supernatural, and holy dwelling place—His Kingdom—is living inside you. You are carrying eternity, a dimension that is far beyond the limits of time. Every single promise in God's Word has been given to us from eternity. Through the power of prayer, you can bring heaven to earth. When Jesus taught the disciples to pray in Matthew 6:10, He told them to pray, "Your kingdom come. Your will be done on earth as it is in heaven." As simple as it may seem, prayer is the vehicle that brings what is in eternity into now. When the Holy Spirit makes you aware of His good plans and purpose for your future, you can begin to pray those things into being. You are, in essence, partnering with God to birth these things into the earth.

Activating your prophetic promise

The word *activate* means to "cause to function."[2] When you activate something, it puts motion or animation to it. A promise from God can be unlocked in part through your comprehension. It's impossible to unlock what you don't understand. Understanding God's prophetic word over your life is key to walking in that word.

This is an area in which the enemy fights against believers. It's his deceptive job to blind people spiritually to the promises of God over their lives. If people don't realize that it's their right to have something, then in ignorance they often forfeit it. As you read this, however, I'm declaring that you will not forfeit the promises of God in your life. They will surely come to pass!

After you understand God's promises, then it's necessary to abide in Him, according to John chapter 15. To abide in Him means to continue, to remain, and to be consistent in following His instructions and ways. Not only must we abide in Him, but His Word must abide in us. This means we must read, study, and meditate on the holy Scriptures. This is done through relationship, not obligation. I read, study, and meditate on the Word because I love God. It's also a necessity. I need the Word in order to live. John 15:7 says, "If you abide in Me, and My words abide in you, you will ask what you desire, and it shall be done for you." Abiding in the Father activates God's future promise and causes it to manifest in your present.

PROPHETIC INTEL

It's time that you understand your prophetic nature. You've been called to speak forth the words of God in the earth. What you say in accordance with the Word of God is backed by heaven. Recognize that the Holy Spirit desires to reveal Himself to you in new ways. He desires to show you revelation of the future. The Bible reveals that "the testimony of Jesus is the spirit of prophecy" (Revelation 19:10). When the Holy Spirit speaks words to you for yourself or others, those words bring edification and comfort, and they bring clear direction, insight, and needed information. When that happens, He is revealing Jesus Christ through you.

It's a powerful thing to know that the Ancient of Days is revealing Himself in you and through you. The only thing you need to do is partner with God to see His plans released in our world. Here are some ways you can partner with Him and unlock your prophetic future:

Fully submit and surrender your life, desires, and path to the Lord:
When you do this, it allows God to flow fully through you, unhindered.

Increase your faith: It takes faith to prophesy, to see in the spiritual realm, or even to hear from God. Increase your faith by reading, reciting, and hearing the Word.

Do your part: In a partnership, there are always two distinct roles. You have a significant part to play in seeing God's plans realized in your life. Your part is obedience. When you obey God and follow His instructions in the natural, He will do that which is above and beyond your ability—the supernatural.

2

God Still Speaks Today

Man shall not live by bread alone, but by every word that comes from
the mouth of God.

Matthew 4:4 ESV

Have you ever wondered if God is trying to communicate a direct message
to you? Do you have an inner knowing that He wants to tell you something,
but you're just unsure if it's Him or if you're making it all up in your head?
If you're there, then I've been exactly where you are. That was me when I
first started a relationship with the Holy Spirit. I thought, *I must be going
crazy; is God really trying to speak to me?*

I was extremely young at that time, and I had no idea that I was just
starting out on the journey of a lifetime. Walking in faith with Jesus will
lead you on an adventure that you never knew you needed, but once you
start, you couldn't imagine your life without. Your faith will be stretched,
your mind will be transformed, and your life will be turned upside down
in the best way. When you are in true relationship with someone, there is
conversation. Communication is not a one-sided experience. Communication is not only speaking, but also hearing as you are being spoken to.

That's a beautiful definition of what prayer is. You speak to God, and He speaks to your heart.

I am totally convinced that God still speaks today—through the sacred Scriptures of the Bible. And from that foundation, I believe that He also speaks through modern-day prophets or seers. Jesus says it this way in Matthew 4:4 (ESV): "Man shall not live by bread alone, but by every word that comes from the mouth of God." This denotes a progression of ongoing communication. God didn't just speak during ancient times; we are still living by the words that He is speaking now. A still, small voice, a tug on the heart, a picture or vision, a dream, or just a simple unexplainable knowing inside us are all ways that He communicates. And you don't have to be a prophet to perceive and know His voice. It's my conviction that every believer carries a prophetic essence in his or her spirit.

There are seven key modes in which God speaks throughout Scripture. We will explore these modes shortly, but first, I'm so intrigued by how the Bible shows the many diversities of the sound of God's voice. His voice is described as the sound of many waters in Revelation 14:2. It's described as thunder in Job 37:2 and Psalm 29:3. The sound of His voice is depicted as mighty in Psalm 68:33. It's explained as a roar in Job 37:4, yet it's also shown as a whisper in 1 Kings 19:12. The voice of the Lord is beautiful in its variety.

God speaks with many sounds in Scripture, in many and various ways. That's still true today. He not only speaks through verbal communication; He also speaks through other unique forms. It's important to understand the modes God uses to speak, so you can be open to how He might want to speak to you. Here are seven key modes He speaks in: (1) through Scripture, (2) in an audible voice, (3) in an impression on the heart, (4) through people, (5) with signs, (6) with visions, and (7) in various types of dreams. These are not the only ways that God speaks. In fact, I give you a more detailed list of the different ways in the "Prophetic Intel" section at the end of chapter 3. But these are the seven key modes I want to look at more closely here.

1. Through Scripture

According to 2 Timothy 3:16–17, Scripture is God-breathed, or inspired. This means that God instructed and inspired men to write His words.

Scripture has supreme authority and is the most important mode by which God speaks. It is the leader and foundation for all the other ways that He communicates with us. In addition, Scripture is the judge that we use to vet dreams, signs, visions, our perceptions, other people's voices, and any of the other ways we believe that God is speaking to us. Because the Spirit and the Word always agree, if a form of communication goes against the written Word of God, then it is not from God.

The Bible reveals the fall of humanity came through sin and human error, yet God's redemption plan comes through His Son, Jesus Christ, bringing restoration. Old and New Testament Scripture reveals Christ, the Messiah, as Savior of the world. Holy Scripture is timeless and speaks to every era, age, society, and civilization in the world.

God is still speaking through each page of the written Word. The early Hebrews viewed the sacred text they had (the Torah) as a loving heavenly Father giving His children instructions for life. The written Word of God is the life-giving source from which we draw strength, direction, comfort, and instruction. Scripture guides us through the difficult situations that we face in our modern world. It is food for our spirit and nourishment for our soul.

God is always speaking through the Bible. For this reason, you should read the Word daily, allowing it to renew your mind, transform your thinking, and restore your heart.

2. In an Audible Voice

Throughout the Bible, God speaks audibly to His people. He is seen as the Father speaking lovingly, instructively, and at times sternly or correctively. At different times, the voice of the Lord can be as loud as a boom to get your attention, or as soft and gentle as a persistent thought. The Holy Spirit desires to speak to your heart, and He may communicate as an internal voice or an external force. Hebrews 4:7 says, "Today, if you will hear His voice, do not harden your hearts." The heart is the centermost part of a person. It's the core of your being that fuels the rest of the entire body. He speaks to your heart, that what He says might reverberate throughout your being. Your heart captures the sound of His voice, and your spirit and soul respond.

In order to hear the Lord's voice, you must open your heart to Him. Jesus desires to communicate with you, but you must fully engage with Him through real relationship—worship. John 4:24 says, "God is Spirit, and those who worship Him must worship in spirit and truth." Spirit to spirit, without hiding or deception, opens the heart to perceive and receive Jesus. When you hear the voice of the Lord, you will realize that you already know it. John 10:4–5 (ESV) says, "And the sheep follow him, for they know his voice. A stranger they will not follow." The Lord's voice is familiar to those who know Him, because the spirit of a person is eternal. We were with God before we were placed here on this earth. As God told Jeremiah, "Before I formed thee in the belly I knew thee" (Jeremiah 1:5 KJV).

The voice of the Lord has several key identifiers that set it apart from any other voice. Here are some attributes that will help you in learning, relearning, and further understanding the voice of God. His voice is:

The voice of truth: God will never speak a lie or anything that goes against His Word, the Bible. In Scripture, the Holy Spirit is called "the Spirit of truth" (John 16:13). He reveals what is hidden, bringing light, justice, and righteousness. His voice of truth brings order to chaos, direction in uncertainty, and freedom where there was bondage.

The voice of love: When God speaks, He overwhelms us with His love. The voice of the Lord comforts, uplifts, and heals. We feel His love through the words He speaks and the reverberations of His sound.

Our compass: The voice of God is our locator. Through it, He is able to find us no matter where we are mentally, emotionally, spiritually, or physically. His voice leads us into the path that we should go, helping us determine our next step, and positioning us for the future.

A rod and staff: The Lord's voice is our correction. Psalm 23:4 depicts the shepherd's rod and staff as tools for discipline. With them, the shepherd keeps the sheep in line and away from unseen dangers.

Likewise, symbolically God uses His voice as a tool to keep us from hidden and unseen danger. His voice is our protective covering.

A shofar: The Lord's voice is the chief trumpet calling His people into divine order. When He speaks, He releases a spiritual alarm to wake up the Church. He warns, instructs, and urgently directs us to walk in the right path. He alerts us to destruction and satanic agendas. In addition, the shofar not only sounds for battle, but also when there is jubilee or times of celebration. God's voice is championing His people into victory.

The voice of wisdom: In Scripture, the Spirit of the Lord is called "the Spirit of wisdom" (Isaiah 11:2). He gives knowledge, instructions, and supernatural insight. Through His voice, He gives us the know-how to be successful in life.

3. In an Impression on the Heart

God often communicates with us heart to heart. This type of communication is not an audible voice, but an inner knowing, a prophetic perception. The word *perceive* means to come to realize or understand. Prophetic perception, or God's impression upon your heart, is when you become spiritually aware of something that you would not have known, except by the Spirit of God.

Second Samuel 5:12 (KJV) says, "And David perceived that the LORD had established him king over Israel, and that he had exalted his kingdom for his people Israel's sake." David *perceived*, and the Hebrew word used there is *yāda*, which means to have recognition and to know.[1]

When God speaks this way, it's so rewarding because you don't have to guess; you just know or perceive what God has done. You sense it in the core of your being. God designed us so that if we are in real relationship with Him, our perception will be directly linked to Him.

4. Through People

The Bible is chock-full of examples of God using various people to release life-giving words from Him to others. Plain and simple, God speaks through people. It has been God's desire to partner with people in the earth to fulfill His will for humanity and the world. Through the gifts of the Spirit, God ignites His divine communication in the hearts of men and women, who are then able to reveal His mysteries.

Prophecy, one of the nine gifts of the Spirit, gives people the ability to hear God through divine inspiration and release those words to other individuals. When aligned with God's heart, people can express extreme compassion, encouragement, and wisdom to others. Those who exude the love of God in this way are revealing His heart to others.

Not only can God speak through the gift of prophecy, but His communication may also come through people as a word of knowledge, another of the nine gifts of the Spirit. (We will talk more about each of the nine gifts in chapter 16's section titled "Intensifying Gifts of the Spirit.") Such words of knowledge provide godly instruction or wisdom, healing, or even the working of miracles (occurrences that defy human or natural understanding or laws).

Be open to the thought that God may desire to use you to speak a life-giving word to someone. It's possible that you may be the human vehicle whom God uses to relay to someone His heart in some way, whether by a life-giving word, a loving warning, or a word of His wisdom. You may just be the answer to someone else's prayer, embodying the voice of God in that person's life for that moment.

5. With Signs

Signs are around us all the time. They are a part of the world systems that govern our day-to-day lives. God crafted the world so that it would show forth signs. Signs are indicators of what's to come. In Luke 21:25, Jesus gives us some examples of natural signs that will occur near the end: "And there will be signs in the sun, in the moon, and in the stars; and on the earth distress of nations, with perplexity, the sea and the waves roaring."

God gives you signs so you can prepare and make the necessary adjustments for what's ahead. Some signs can even cause you to avoid danger completely just by following simple instructions.

Think about some of the road signs we follow when driving. For example, a STOP sign is placed at an intersection to keep cars from colliding and people from getting seriously injured. According to traffic regulations, a STOP sign is in the category of a warning sign. It gives you an immediate perception that danger is near if you don't stop.

There are spiritual signs all around us, and even signs in the sky and earth, that reveal to us that God exists and that He is lovingly communicating with us.

6. With Visions

All throughout the chapters ahead, I describe various visions that the Lord has given me to share with you. By the end of the book, you will therefore have a good idea of how visions come and what they might look like. Let me just say that visions can show up as a mental picture or an image in the mind. They can even look as vivid as a scene from a movie playing out right in front of you.

A vision differs from a dream in that you are wide awake when you happen to see into the realm of the Spirit through a vision. In the Bible, God often connects dreams and visions together. They are a similar form of communication. God dreams are pictures, scenes, or glimpses of the future given when you are asleep. Visions can be pictures, scenes, or glimpses of the future given when you are awake. The types of dreams I discuss in the next section can also be used to describe types of visions.

Here are a couple of Scriptures that show God speaking about giving visions and dreams to His people:

> "Hear now My words: If there is a prophet among you, I, the LORD, make Myself known to him in a vision; I speak to him in a dream" (Numbers 12:6).

> "In the last days, God says, I will pour out my Spirit on all people. Your sons and daughters will prophesy, your young men will see visions, your old men will dream dreams" (Acts 2:17 NIV).

God gives people visions of what is to come. The visions may reveal His plan, or may involve a situation regarding someone's future, a personal communication from Him to you, a warning of impeding danger, or even a future world event.

7. In Various Types of Dreams

Do you know that you will spend one-third of your life asleep? This means that by the time you are sixty years of age, twenty years of your life will have been spent sleeping. There must be a reason God would have us sleep for one-third of our lives. It's a fact that sleep refreshes and rejuvenates the body, but it also provides humankind with a direct line into another world. There is a world beyond this world, a realm beyond this realm, that is a component of the spiritual world. I call it the dream world.

Throughout the Scriptures, it's evident that God uses dreams to speak to His people. It's believed that one-third of the Bible deals with dreams— either a dream itself, the interpretation, or some event pertaining to it. Oftentimes, God will place encrypted messages within dreams that can only be revealed through a person with the gift of interpretation. Although God uses dreams to speak to His people, it's important to realize that not all dreams are from God. Some may be from the soul of a person. Even demonic spirits can infiltrate dreams.

A dream from God is going to communicate His love, His word, His instruction, His warning, or His correction. Job 33:14–16 says, "For God may speak in one way, or in another, yet man does not perceive it. In a dream, in a vision of the night, when deep sleep falls upon men, while slumbering on their beds, then He opens the ears of men, and seals their instruction." Some translations of verse 16 say, "terrifying them with warnings." God warns of impending danger.

Below are several types of dreams found in Scripture. This list will help you decode what you see in the realm of the night.

Dreams of prophecy

A dream of prophecy is receiving images, sounds, thoughts, and/or sensations during sleep that give foreknowledge of what is to come. This foreknowledge could pertain to someone's personal life or even an entire group of people, such as a nation.

Matthew 1:20 provides a great example of a prophetic dream. It gives insight into the lives of Joseph and Mary, the mother of Jesus. At this particular point, Mary was espoused to Joseph, promised to him in marriage. In our society, this would be similar to an engagement. During the time of their engagement, Mary was found pregnant. Of course, we know that it was an immaculate conception. In Joseph's mind, however, he had more than likely determined that she had been intimate with someone else. Although he was upset, he was a good-hearted man and didn't plan on humiliating her publicly. Scripture indicates that he planned to put her away privately.

But God visited Joseph in a dream by sending an angel to appear to him. In the dream, this angel of the Lord exclaimed, "Do not fear to take Mary as your wife, for that which is conceived in her is from the Holy Spirit" (Matthew 1:20 ESV). The angel assured Joseph, "She will bear a son, and you shall call his name Jesus, for he will save his people from their sins" (verse 21). This prophetic dream guided the young couple and brought clarity for their future. In this same manner, a dream of prophecy can do likewise for you today.

Dreams that reveal callings

One way God may reveal your calling is through your dreams. Oftentimes, dreams can reflect the will of God for your life. In 2 Peter 1:10, Peter instructs believers to acknowledge and be sure of the calling God gives them: "Therefore, brethren, be even more diligent to make your call and election sure, for if you do these things you will never stumble." Many people overcomplicate what their calling is. Some think that a calling has to be this grand, extravagant destiny. In its simplest form, your calling is simply what you are born to do on this earth. Your calling is your life's mission. It's how you help others while bringing glory to God.

Dreams that reveal purpose or callings are laced throughout Scripture. Through a sequence of dreams, God showed the Old Testament dreamer Joseph his calling and future position:

He said to them, "Hear this dream that I have dreamed: Behold, we were binding sheaves in the field, and behold, my sheaf arose and stood upright. And behold, your sheaves gathered around it and bowed down to my sheaf." His brothers said to him, "Are you indeed to reign over us? Or are you indeed to rule over us?" So they hated him even more for his dreams and for his words.

Genesis 37:6–8 ESV

This dream Joseph had was one in a sequence of dreams that revealed his calling to him. Joseph was called to serve in a position of great authority and power. He was called to serve as second-in-command to Pharaoh. God was relaying this to Joseph through symbolic dreams that depicted him being elevated and seated in a position of power. Sure enough, all of Joseph's brothers had to come and bow down to him during the later famine, just as the dreams depicted. These were dreams of calling that shed light on the destiny God had given Joseph. Although it would be years before Joseph actually saw the dreams fulfilled, they served as a beacon of light to propel him on his journey in life.

Dreams of correction and discipline

One of the main assignments the Holy Spirit has on this earth is to correct you and keep you in line with the will of God. According to Hebrews 12:6, the Lord disciplines those He loves. Correction is a sign of His unconditional love for us. Now, we're not always sensitive to the reproof our heavenly Father gives, or willing to listen. So I've learned that when God can't get our attention while we're awake, the best opportunity He may have is when we're in a relaxed, somewhat immobilized state. People are usually the most relaxed when they're asleep. For this reason, when you're sleeping God may take the opportunity to deal with your heart through a dream of correction.

Genesis 20 gives us a biblical example of a dream of correction and reproof. Abraham travels to and settles in a place called Gerar, on the southern border of Canaan. This was a wealthy place with prosperous pastures. At that time, Gerar was under the rule of King Abimelech. For

28

fear of Gerar's people and practices, Abraham wanted to conceal the truth that he and his wife, Sarah, were married. To protect her and also himself, he said that Sarah was his sister. By speaking this deception and presenting her as a single woman who hadn't borne any children, Abraham imperiled her purity. Although Sarah was ninety at the time, she apparently was a beautiful woman. So King Abimelech took Sarah for himself.

Unknowingly, Abimelech was at fault for planning to take another man's wife. He had not yet touched Sarah, but it was certainly in his heart to do so. This was very displeasing to God, and it would bring a curse upon Abimelech and the nation he governed. Scripture reveals that God therefore visited Abimelech in a dream by night and showed him the error of his ways. This swift rebuke to Abimelech is an example of a dream of correction and reproof. God sent a dream of correction to him before he actually committed the repugnant deed, telling him, "I also withheld you from sinning against Me; therefore I did not let you touch her" (Genesis 20:6). When God sends this type of dream, it can literally keep you from sinning against Him. Abimelech was presented with two options. The first was to restore Abraham's wife to him. Because Abraham was a prophet, he would then pray for Abimelech and the king would live. The second option was to keep Sarah for himself. If he did this, however, then God told him the consequence would be his own destruction (see verse 7). Because of the dream, Abimelech chose the first option!

Dreams of knowledge

In 1 Corinthians 12:8, the apostle Paul begins to reveal the gifts of the Spirit. The second spiritual gift or endowment that he speaks of is the word of knowledge. The Greek word for knowledge is *gnosis*, which means supernatural intelligence or understanding.[2] The word of knowledge is a gift that gives some people the ability to perceive things by divine dispensation. With the gift of knowledge, a person receives information and facts concerning things that he or she had no previous knowledge of. This is an extraordinary gift that is often used for revealing the secrets and desires of someone's heart in order to win that individual to Christ (see 1 Corinthians 14:24–25).

The gift of knowledge can also come in the form of a dream. I call these dreams of knowledge. By supernatural means, they reveal to you what's taking place. They may also give you intelligence or understanding about matters that you had no natural perception of. The gift of knowledge is different from the gift of prophecy in that it is not foretelling the future. The gift of knowledge gives information on what's happening now, or what presently exists.

With knowledge of something also come instructions. God never gives you such knowledge without instructions. Dreams of knowledge can come in the form of God giving insight on a matter and telling you what to do. One of the definitions of *knowledge* is awareness—having a perception of a situation or becoming well-informed about a situation or development.

Dreams of warning

Dreams of warning can help you avoid impending danger. This is another very common type of dream that we see in the Bible. God cares so much for His people that He gives dreams to express His caution or concern about a decision or path they might take.

God is the type of father who will not force you to do anything, but He has vested in you the greatest power that there is—the power of choice! Because our lives are constantly driven by choices, God gives us warning dreams as a guide. Many people are so busy and caught up with the everyday tasks life brings that prayer is often forgotten. For this reason, God may speak to you in a dream, warning you about a decision you are getting ready to make, or have already made.

Dreams of inventions and ideas

God is such a creative mastermind! Creativity simply exudes from Him. He singlehandedly crafted the earth and billions of galaxies. He positioned the stars and aligned the constellations. He divided the firmament and created every living organism and non-living thing with the release of His words. All of which He spun from His vast imagination, bringing it into our reality. He formed humankind from some of the smallest particles of the earth, known as dust. Then He breathed His breath into us!

The word *breathe* literally means to inspire. To inspire is to fill with the urge or ability to do something. Dreams may come in the form of an idea or invention. This is a type of dream that comes straight from the mind of God and connects to the creative nature He placed inside you! God may give you a dream about an idea or invention that would unlock the door to your future.

In Genesis 41, after having disturbing dreams, Pharaoh seeks out Joseph for God's interpretation. This is very interesting because God had given Pharaoh a dream of warning about what was to come. As I discussed in the previous point, warning dreams come so that you can prepare and make the right decision. I'm discussing Pharaoh's particular dream now because from what I see, it's a combination of the two types of dreams. Out of Pharaoh's warning dream, God gives Joseph not only an interpretation, but also an idea and invention. Joseph tells Pharaoh,

> They should collect all the food of these good years that are coming and store up the grain under the authority of Pharaoh, to be kept in the cities for food. This food should be held in reserve for the country, to be used during the seven years of famine that will come upon Egypt, so that the country may not be ruined by the famine.
>
> Genesis 41:35–36 NIV

An invention is "a new useful process, machine, improvement, etc., that did not exist previously and that is recognized as the product of some unique intuition or genius."[3] In this passage of Scripture, God gives Joseph an invention—a new, useful process and improvement that did not exist in that country previously. The idea God gives is to set up an international storehouse. This concept had not entered the mind of Pharaoh or any of his chief advisors before that time. This is why they needed Joseph's expertise and the divine idea from God. From the interpretation of Pharoah's dream, Joseph received God's wisdom and created a massive storehouse that saved the nation of Egypt and also those from other nations who received help over the seven years of famine.

| PROPHETIC INTEL |

God still speaks today, and He wants to speak to you. The sound of His voice and the ways He speaks are many and varied, as we talked about in this chapter. Don't limit the ways God wants to speak to you, or how He may want to speak through you. If you're a dreamer, embrace that, yet also open yourself up to other ways He may communicate with you. Likewise, if you see visions, don't always think that God may show you things that way. Take the limits off, and you will begin to know Him in a deeper way. Here are seven steps to help you activate your ability to hear from God:

1. Grab pen and notebook to capture the words of God (smart-phones and digital devices can be quite distracting, which is why I use old-fashioned paper and ink).
2. Pray and ask the Lord what's on His heart for you. Communicate with Him fervently.
3. Praise and worship Him.
4. Read a Scripture from the Bible that speaks to your spirit.
5. After praying, reading Scripture, and worshiping God, stop and listen quietly in His presence.
6. Take your notebook and begin to write what you hear, believe, or perceive God is saying to you.
7. Ask yourself, *Does what I heard agree with the Bible?* God will never speak contrary to His written Word.

3

It Might Sound Crazy, but I'm Hearing God

And I heard a voice from heaven, like the voice of many waters, and like the voice of loud thunder.

Revelation 14:2

Some of the things I've heard from God that I'm going to share with you in the next several chapters may seem farfetched; they may even be startling or hard to believe. Throughout the years, I've learned that God will speak to you of a future that does not yet exist in your world. Your natural mind may unknowingly fight God's words because you've never seen that reality. He may speak something that has never entered into your heart or mind.

My journey of hearing the voice of God and receiving messages from Him started as a young child. When I was young, I thought I had to be crazy to think that God could actually speak to me. But it wasn't long before He proved Himself in the most amazing ways. (I'll get into some of that later.)

I was a 1980s baby and grew up in the '90s, before so much of the world changed in the early 2000s. There were no smartphones, flat-screen TVs, or social media sites. I mean, the internet didn't even exist. I'd come home from school and rush to go outside and play with friends. Anything we could find in our environment was fair game to create a game or have fun. We'd use sticks, rocks, old tires, metal bars, or anything else we could get our hands on.

One of my favorite things to do as a child was watch TV. Saturday cartoons were the best. I'd wake up in the morning as early as I could, and run and grab a bowl of cereal that was 60 percent Froot Loops and 40 percent milk. It was the perfect ratio for a relaxing Saturday. I remember the TV not having the best signal. My brothers and I would take the antenna setup we called rabbit ears and adjust them to get the right signal. The TV would flicker with static. You could only see part of the show going in and out. A word or two would come across, and then loud static noise. I quickly learned how to position the antenna just right to see a clear picture. My aunt taught me how to place aluminum foil on the rabbit ears to get the best results. This hack brought me hours of endless entertainment throughout my early childhood years.

My family and I were middle-class poor. We didn't have much, but we were resourceful with what we had. We used foil on anything. The TV signal would kick right back in with it. Like the TV, the radio was also tricky to tune in. Riding in the car, you'd have to turn the dial to the right frequency to pick up the radio signal. If you didn't, your favorite tunes would sound inaudible, as if you were listening to them underwater. It was then that I learned the importance of connecting to the right channel or frequency. If you grew up before the 2000s, then you also remember what it was like riding in your car and trying to get a clear radio signal as you searched through the different frequencies or channels to find your favorite station.

God's Divine Frequency

Picking up the right frequency made all the difference. A radio frequency refers to the frequency band that transmits wireless telecommunication signals. In scientific terms, *radio frequency* (RF) refers to "the rate of oscillation of electromagnetic radio waves in the range of 3 kHz to 300 GHz, as well as the alternating currents carrying the radio signals."[1] In physics, *frequency* is "the number of waves that pass a fixed point in unit time; also, the number of cycles or vibrations undergone during one unit of time by a body in periodic motion."[2] Even today, electronics still have these signals; we just can't see or hear them. The electronic transmitters in our devices are still emitting waves on different frequencies; we just don't need rabbit ears to pick them up.

I believe that there is a frequency, a wavelength, on which God transmits His divine communications with us. I am of the belief that He is always speaking; people just are not always in a place to listen. In Isaiah 55:8–9 (ESV), God speaks a powerful mystery: "For my thoughts are not your thoughts, neither are your ways my ways, declares the LORD. For as the heavens are higher than the earth, so are my ways higher than your ways and my thoughts than your thoughts." In these verses, God separates Himself from human thoughts and ways. He uses the Hebrew word *gabahh*, which we translate as higher. It means upward, raised up, a great height, and exalted.[3] It comes from a primitive root word meaning to soar. God's thoughts are so superior, vast, and beyond our intellect that they are soaring above our heads like electronic signals being transmitted. The only way to capture this divine communication is to have your receptors positioned to receive it.

Out of God's mercy, compassion, and enormous grace, He descends to us. Yet He still requires us to elevate our minds, hearts, and thinking to fully receive Him. This is connected to the word *repent* in Scripture. Acts 3:19 says, "Repent therefore and be converted." To repent is to change your mind and thinking. It is putting away sin and those things that are unprofitable for your soul. Then and only then can you be converted, which means being adapted to a new purpose or being made suitable for it. When God converts your soul, He gives you into your higher calling. Repentance gives us the ability to tap into God's divine frequency.

Elijah was used to hearing God in a certain way. Because of Elijah's calling and relationship with the Lord, God would speak to him in the grandest ways. Elijah had an interesting connection with the elements, nature, and the things in his environment. God would speak to Elijah by stirring up a massive fire. Or Elijah would hear God in a storm-forced wind. Then there were times when he heard God in an enormous earthquake that shattered the Richter scale. At this point in his life, however, he was in a transition.

It was a turning point in his journey, where each move he made would be vitally significant, as God would soon take him to heaven in a chariot of fire (see 2 Kings 2:11).

Before that transpired, however, he found himself on the run from a witch by the name of Jezebel. One day, she made an announcement that she would take his life and that he would dead by the same time the next day:

> Then Jezebel sent a messenger to Elijah, saying, "So let the gods do to me, and more also, if I do not make your life as the life of one of them [the slaughtered prophets of Baal] by tomorrow about this time." And when he saw that, he arose and ran for his life.
>
> 1 Kings 19:2–3

Pay attention to verse 3. Jezebel released a word curse of death against Elijah, and the Bible says when he *saw* that, he ran for his life. This means that the words of Jezebel affected his vision. He saw (visualized and formed a mental picture of) her taking his life. Every word or voice operates on a frequency or wavelength. When your mind is unguarded or unrenewed, it will embrace low-level frequencies like demonic words, negativity, gossip, and division. Because Elijah had a momentary lapse, he allowed the words of this idolatrous woman to enter his mind and heart, to the point that he saw what she said.

If you're going to live and commune on God's frequency, you must go higher. You must drown out the negativity, demonic chatter, and fleshly impulses so you can truly receive from the Father. It's also possible that based on the season you're in, God may shift the frequency of the way in which He communicates with you. If you're used to hearing Him one way, you must be so in tune with the Holy Spirit that if He's coming to you in a new way, you're spiritually aware enough to pick Him up on that new frequency.

Elijah ran into the wilderness out of fear for his life. He searched for God in all of the normal ways that he was used to hearing Him. But the frequency had changed. In 1 Kings 19:11–12 (ESV), Elijah picks up on the new signal:

> And he [God] said, "Go out, and stand on the mount before the LORD." And behold, the LORD passed by, and a great and strong wind tore the mountains

and broke in pieces the rocks before the LORD, but the LORD was not in the wind. And after the wind an earthquake, but the LORD was not in the earthquake. And after the earthquake a fire, but the LORD was not in the fire. And after the fire the sound of a low whisper.

Instead of the fire, wind, and earthquake, God came to Elijah in a still, small voice, a simple whisper. When life and your circumstances are loud, God's voice may sound like a whisper. You must learn to quiet your world in order to truly hear Him.

God's frequency is wherever His presence is. You can find Him in any situation, storm, or circumstance. You can locate Him with a simple prayer, a tear, a cry of *I need you, Lord*. When you call on the name of Jesus Christ, He has promised He will be there. The Spirit of the Lord is everywhere, waiting for an opportunity to speak to your heart, hear your cry, and walk with you through life. In the same way that there are millions of signals and electronic transmissions going on around us, there are also millions of voices, impulses, and detractors vying for our attention. Those frequencies, from media to your friends and family, are easy to hear. Everyone has a thought, opinion, or voice. As 1 Corinthians 14:10 (KJV) says, "There are, it may be, so many kinds of voices in the world, and none of them is without signification." What's even more significant is the frequency that you tune your hearing to. The voice that you give your ear to is the voice that controls you.

Things That Block Spiritual Signals

Many factors can stop clear communication. Bad reception could hinder a clear signal. Spiritually, people could have something in their lives that hinders them from clearly receiving from God. Growing up, I had to wrestle with the radio antenna, constantly changing its direction until I could get good reception. Likewise, a person may have to reposition his or her spiritual posture or receiver in order to hear from God clearly.

Hidden sin in your heart can block spiritual communication. It takes purity to unblock the signal. It's important always to keep a heart of repentance toward God. Sometimes without even realizing it, you may have done some things that possibly offended the Holy Spirit. The more you grow in your love for God, the more you will develop sensitivity to what grieves Him and what pleases Him. Being free from sin puts you on a frequency to hear the voice of the Lord clearly.

Let's take a closer look at the life of Samuel: "And the child Samuel ministered unto the LORD before Eli. And the word of the LORD was precious in those days; there was no open vision" (1 Samuel 3:1 KJV). This verse indicates that Samuel ministered to the Lord before Eli in a period in biblical history when there was no open vision. In other words, revelation had been shut up. There was no fresh word; there was no progressive revelation. In fact, the priest Eli couldn't even see, because his eyes had begun to wax dim. This is a reference to both his natural and spiritual sight. The word *vision* in the verse is the Hebrew word *chazown*, meaning divine communication.[4] Heaven was not speaking to earth. God chose a boy named Samuel, who would become a great prophet, to change this.

Yet at first, "Samuel did not yet know the LORD, nor had the word of the LORD yet been revealed to him" (1 Samuel 3:7 NASB). This verse of Scripture enlightened me. It shows that you can be called into prophetic ministry and even minister in the house of God, yet still not know the Lord. To know Him is to have an intimate relationship with Him. Samuel served in God's house before the word of the Lord was ever revealed to him, and before he received an open vision. I believe that Samuel could not speak as an oracle of God until he had first served. Serving is foundational and postures you, like an antenna, to be aligned with the signal of heaven.

Samuel also represented a pure vessel being sanctified and set apart. He represented prophetic purity returning to Israel. When purity comes into your life, it will help you tune in a clear frequency to hear the words of the Lord. It's also possible, however, to be tuned in to a spiritual channel or frequency that is not of God. The spirit world can be much like an atmosphere full of radio waves. If you feed your spirit with things that are not godly, those things have your ear. In this case, it's important to *change the frequency!* Shift from dark communication to receiving the light of God.

I'm using the analogy of signals and radio frequencies to explain simply some ways that you can be blocked from properly communicating with God. The point is to remove all barriers to communication. Here are six communication barriers psychologists and experts in the business world have identified. Identifying these in our own lives can also help us spiritually:

1. *Filtering* is the distortion or withholding of information in order to manage reactions and change responses. In the spiritual, it's imperative to hear God without adding or taking away from His written Word or spoken word. When you filter what He says through your own mind and emotions, you will always misconstrue His heart and intentions.

2. *Selective perception* refers to filtering what we see and hear to suit our own needs. This process is often unconscious. The way you were raised, or even your experiences in life, can cause you to have selective perception or reception.

3. *Information overload,* or receiving too much information in a limited time, can be defined as "occurring when the information processing demands on an individual's time to perform interactions and internal calculations exceed the supply or capacity of time available for such processing."[5] When your life is too cluttered and there are too many voices in your ear, it's impossible to hear from the Lord. As human beings, we have limited capacity to take in information. If the voice of God is not activating you, then another voice is.

4. *Emotional disconnects* happen when a person is upset, whether about a current subject or about some unrelated incident that may have happened. Life situations and circumstances can cause warfare, emotionally disconnecting a person from God. The way to combat becoming emotionally disconnected is to feed on the Word of God and spend time worshiping Him. This strengthens your faith through emotionally turbulent times.

5. *Lack of source familiarity or credibility* is sharing information without a proper foundation or relationship with the receiver. In the business world, one example is trying to have personal conversation (whether serious or even joking) with someone who doesn't know you well. Spiritually speaking, when we don't have a relationship with God, we cannot expect to speak to Him as if we do. It's important to know your source. If you want to hear from God, get to know Him.

6. *Semantics* is the study of meaning in communication. Words can mean different things to different people, or a word might not mean anything to another person. When it comes to having a close relationship with the Holy Spirit, the Bible teaches us how to pray and communicate with Him. We are to pray His words back to Him. When you pray, remind Him of the promises He has given to you (see Isaiah 62:6).

Removing any barriers to communication with God will allow you to hear from Him properly and posture yourself in alignment with heaven.

PROPHETIC INTEL

God still speaks today, and He wants to speak to you. The ways He speaks are many. Earlier we read Revelation 14:2, a verse that denotes the power and multiplicity of the various sounds of His voice, such as the voice of many waters. Because God speaks in various ways, it's imperative that you don't limit the ways He wants to speak to you. Think of the many ways He communicates with you and identify them. What ways are you used to hearing God? What ways do you need to be more open in order to hear Him? To help you process this, here is a list of some of the ways He speaks:

- Holy Scriptures
- Visions
- Dreams
- Impressions on the heart
- Perception
- Through people you meet
- Imagery
- Preaching of the Word
- Supernatural knowing
- Mental pictures
- Through signs or wonders
- Nature and the environment
- Numbers
- Trials or experiences
- Books or writings
- Audible voice
- A whisper
- A thought
- A voice in your heart/mind
- Colors or symbols
- Challenges or life lessons

God has created so many ways to get through to our spirits in order to get His valuable words to us. The more you embrace that God loves you so much that He wants to communicate with you as a friend, the more you will begin to see Him in everything. Matthew 5:8 says, "Blessed are the pure in heart, for they shall see God." The more your heart is purified, the more you will see and hear God.

4

God Speaks through Numb3rs

Indeed, the very hairs of your head are all numbered . . .

Luke 12:7 NIV

I blurted out this seemingly random date six months ahead to a couple one time. The word of the Lord for them was "6.29.2010—your life will change forever; you will conceive a child." I had no idea that for nearly twenty years prior, this couple had been unable to have a child. It was at that time in my ministry that I began to see numbers—sometimes as dates, sometimes as spans of time. It felt a bit overwhelming as my prophetic gift of knowledge in this area was growing rapidly. I could see numbers in visions, or over people as I looked at them. Then God would speak an encouraging word of what would occur or what the numbers meant. The lady I ministered to with that specific date gave the testimony later that after she and her doctors had thought she could never have a child, twenty years later God did allow her to conceive, just as the word of the Lord had been given.

On another occasion, I remember releasing a word to a lady while I could see her bank account number. Hold on—I know that sounds odd and highly confidential. I agree, but God can be that detailed if He desires to get information through to a person. He has to be able to trust you if He's going to use you at that level. Familiar spirits, psychics, and others can do something similar, but their source, motive, and intent are different. When it's truly of God, it will point people back to Jesus. Likewise, God won't have a person build his or her entire ministry off such occurrences. These kinds of prophetic signs simply build people's faith and show them that God cares and is more real than they could imagine.

When I see or hear information prophetically, my natural mind is some-how suspended so that the Holy Spirit can flow freely through my spirit. This means that my mind is not processing or filtering what's being shared. For some reason, after a prophecy or word of knowledge is released, I don't normally remember it. I don't recall about 90 percent of the per-sonal prophecies I've given. National or corporate prophecies are quite different. These are words that God reveals for regions or nations, which affect the course of the future. Those things can be seared into my mind for many years.

I shared the numbers that I saw in the Spirit with this lady, and I told her it was a bank account she had. Then God showed me a check with an American flag on it that was connected to the account. In a skeptical yet intrigued way, this woman pulled out her checkbook and examined it carefully. Then she shouted, "Yes, that's me! My personal checks have an American flag on them!" Her excitement was palpable. She looked closer to see if the number I gave was the account number, and she let out a shrill scream: "Yes, that's my account number!"

The Lord further spoke that there was an issue going on with the ac-count, and that she was to call the bank so it would be resolved. In addition, the Lord revealed that there would be a supernatural release of funds into that account, which would bring the provision she desperately needed.

The woman was puzzled because she was not aware of anything being wrong with the account. Because it was after hours, she had to wait to call the bank until the next day. She called and received word that the account had been compromised. The bank worked with her to resolve and restore the account. The word of the Lord then came to pass, and she found su-pernatural provision in that exact bank account.

Are Numbers Speaking to Us?

From the Old Testament to the New Testament, numbers are a significant theme throughout Scripture. God uses numbers, cycles, intervals, dates, and spans of time to release prophecy or a message. Leviticus 23:15–16 (ESV) says,

> You shall count seven full weeks from the day after the Sabbath, from the day that you brought the sheaf of the wave offering. You shall count fifty days to the day after the seventh Sabbath. Then you shall present a grain offering of new grain to the LORD.

God is speaking here of the celebration of Pentecost. He breaks the span into seven intervals of seven. These numbers are no coincidence. We will go further into the meaning behind numbers shortly, but first let's talk about how they relate to the language of Scripture. Hebrew is the language of the early Jews, God's chosen people. Hebrew has been said to be the very language of creation. In fact, a good portion of the Bible was written in this ancient language. Whenever you want to look deeper into the meaning of the Old Testament passages you read in English, you can look to find the Hebrew meaning. Why? Because it's the original language in which the passages were written.

The Hebrew alphabet is known as the *aleph-bet*. In the Hebrew, each letter of the *aleph-bet* has a numerical value. Every letter is assigned a number. In addition, every letter is represented by a word. Therefore, in the Hebrew every number has a significant meaning. The Hebrew letters are also assigned a specific part of the body, which brings even deeper meaning to the numbers. This is very different from the English language. In English, 1 means 1 and 2 means 2. Numbers come from the language of creation, however, and these numbers speak volumes.

I am completely convinced that God created numbers to speak to us. In this chapter, we will explore the first ten letters of the Hebrew *aleph-bet*. The first ten letters have the values 1–10. There is no representation for zero. Anytime zero is present, it represents balance. In mathematics, zero is known for balancing out equations. For multiple digit numbers, the individual meanings are combined. Repeating numbers like 333 or 222 emphasize and amplify the meaning of a single number.

As we explore each number, I adjure you to open up your spiritual eyes and see how it relates to you and your surroundings. For instance, God may emphasize one part of the meaning of a number that relates to you and your situation. I would suggest that you go through your dreams, visions, and impressions to look for numbers. God often speaks to His people through what we would consider insignificant things. For example, you may have seen three angels in a dream or vision. I'm certain the angels were significant, but did you ever think that God might be using the number 3 to speak to you as well? Remember not to overlook the small details.

The Number 1

The Hebrew letter assigned to the number 1 is *alef*. It is the first letter of the Hebrew alphabet, or *aleph-bet*. It is called the *aleph-bet* because the first two letters are *alef* and *beit*. The letter *alef* represents the oneness of God. Oneness is the fact or state of being unified or whole. Oneness also means identity or harmony with or of someone or thing.[1] Identity is simply who you are. That is why the letter *alef* represents God's identity. He is one, whole and unified.

The letter *alef* is especially significant to the Jewish people. It's important because the letter *alef* begins the name of Esther the queen. She's the one whose prayers and intervention saved the Jews from wicked Haman. The number 1 therefore represents God's ability to unite. In this case, God used Esther to unite an entire race and restore them from impending death.

Furthermore, the letter *alef* has three different meanings. The first is *ukt, aluf*, which means chief or master. Chief is a ruler, leader, or head. Master comes from the Latin word *magister* (*magis*), which means more important. All points direct us back to God, who is our master, chief, and most important one. The second meaning of *alef* is *vbpkut, ulfana*. This means a school of learning or teacher. This is very interesting. It denotes a period of learning and gaining much knowledge. It symbolizes the seasons in your life where you are meant to learn from experiences and life lessons. Now, the third meaning of *alef* is taken from the backward spelling of the word *tkp, pela*. It means wondrous. Wondrous denotes something phenomenal that takes place. It expresses the wonders of creation. This goes back to the beginning, when God first created heavens and earth.

Genesis 1:1 says, "In the beginning God (prepared, formed, fashioned, and) created the heavens and the earth" (AMPC). This further denotes that the number 1's meaning insinuates the first or beginning of a thing. From this Scripture, we can gather that this first number represents God's ability to prepare, form, fashion, and create. All of these attributes are compacted into the number 1. If God has impressed this number on your spirit, then you may be in a season of God making you whole. This may be a season where you are being prepared and fashioned for something great.

The body part assigned to the letter *alef* is the upper torso, particularly the chest and respiratory system. This system provides the energy needed by the cells of the body. The primary purpose of the respiratory system is to supply the blood with oxygen, allowing the blood to deliver oxygen to all of the parts of the body. The respiratory system does this simply through our breathing. Spiritually, this represents life. The presence of God is the oxygen in which we need to live.

The Number 2

The Hebrew letter assigned to the number 2 is *beit*. This is the second letter of the Hebrew *aleph-bet*. The letter *beit* comes from the word that means house. This refers to God's house or temple, which indeed is also your body. First Corinthians 6:19 states, "Do you not know that your body is the temple of the Holy Spirit who is in you, whom you have from God, and you are not your own?" This Scripture tells us that we are God's spiritual temples, God's dwelling place. His temple is the place where His glory resides. His temple is within you.

The letter *beit* also represents the soul of a person—the emotions, mind, and human will. The letter *beit* has a numeral value in Hebrew that translates to the word *taavah*, which means desire or passion. (I know this may be a bit complex, but remember that letters in Hebrew have specific definition, meaning, and numbers connected to them. Everything in this language of creation has layered expression.) *Taavah* can denote a negative human property; however, it can also denote positive passion. This information indicates that the number 2 can represent human desires and passions, whether negative or positive. Psalm 37:4 says, "Delight yourself also in the LORD, and He shall give you the desires of your heart." So if God has been resounding the number 2 within your spirit, He may be letting you know that He is granting you your heart's desires.

The specific body part given to this letter *beit* is the right eye, which represents spiritual discernment. This is your ability to see in the Spirit. Discernment is the ability to perceive and recognize. It comes from the Latin word *discernere*, which literally means "to separate." Discernment is therefore your ability to separate between what's good and bad, right and wrong. Furthermore, if God has impressed the number 2 in your spirit, He could be dealing with your perception or judgment. You must know how to discern between what's authentic and what's false.

In addition, the number 2 represents the gift of wisdom. The English definition of wisdom is the quality of having experience, knowledge, and good judgment. It is also the soundness of a decision or action with regard to the application of such experience, knowledge, and good judgment.

I'm sure you didn't realize that all of this was enclosed within the number 2. Numbers are sometimes not what they appear to be. There is more to the number 2 than what meets the eye!

The Number 3

The letter in the Hebrew assigned to the number 3 is *gimmel*. This letter means reward and punishment. This Hebrew word is derived from the word *gemul*, which means both the giving of reward, as well as the giving of punishment. In the Torah or instructions of God, both reward and punishment have the same goal. The ultimate aim is the rectification of the soul to merit or receive God's light to the fullest extent. This reward and punishment mean that people are free to choose between good and evil.

I'm reminded of Jesus, who had the choice between being crucified or passing on the whole experience. He knew that it was a mixture of reward and punishment. He was taking on the punishment for the sins of the world. The ultimate reward, however, was the salvation of the world. Many people only see the number 3 as resurrection, but it is so much more. It represents your ability to choose that which punishes you now, but benefits you in the end.

In the Hebrew, the letter *gimmel* symbolizes a camel, bridge, weaning, and benevolence. A camel is said to represent your journey through this world. The bridge represents a connection from one place to another. Weaning represents a period of growth and maturity. Benevolence represents your ability to give beyond measure, just as Jesus gave His life.

The number 3 can also represent balance and stability. Balance means an even distribution of weight enabling someone or something to remain upright, while stability means firmly established. So if God has been showing you the number 3, He may be making you aware that He is balancing and establishing you.

The body part given to the letter *gimmel* is the right ear, which represents your ability to hear God's instructions. It's also scientifically proven that the ears help balance the body. God therefore reiterates that He is balancing you once again. Anytime God brings attention to the right side of the body, it denotes a strong authoritative force or command. The right ear further implies God speaking His authoritative instructions to you.

Finally, the number 3 also represents the gift of wealth. This is the part of *gimmel* that deals with the reward. Wealth can deal with all aspects of life. It definitely covers finances or money, yet it can also represent having spiritual wealth. Spiritual wealth is being enriched in peace, joy, and fulfillment.

The Number 4

The Hebrew letter given to the number 4 is *dalet*. Hebrew letters are also their own distinct words, and the word *dalet* means door. A door always represents an opportunity. A door is the passageway to accessing a new dimension. It represents a new realm of influence. This word also deals with your ability to choose the right (God-given) opportunity. This letter brings about the awareness that it is God who gives you the power to achieve success. Deuteronomy 8:18 (NIV) declares, "But remember the Lord your God, for it is he who gives you the ability to produce wealth, and so confirms his covenant, which he swore to your ancestors, as it is today." We must always be aware that it is God who gives us the ability to achieve and produce.

The letter *dalet* also represents selflessness. The meaning of selflessness is being concerned more with the needs and wishes of others than with one's own. Deep within this old saying reveals an important message: "What you make happen for others, God will make happen for you." It's your selflessness that creates new doors of opportunity for you.

This letter *dalet* and number 4 are also associated with progeny. The word *progeny* means a descendant, or the descendants of a person. It means offspring. The number 4 therefore reiterates God's promises for your children. God has the ability to reverse the outlook of your children's future. No matter how grim things get, God remembers His promises. Remember that the number 4 represents the open door!

The Number 5

The Hebrew letter assigned to the number 5 is *hei*. This letter represents expression, whether in thought, speech, or action. It expresses the revelation of self in the act of giving oneself to another. Self-expression is giving to others.

The name of the letter *hei* is found in Genesis 47:24, where Joseph was given godly wisdom on what to do in the midst of famine and told people to take seed (*hei*) for themselves. The Jewish people believe that this letter means to "take seed for yourselves." Seed represents resources, food, and so much more. During biblical times, humanity's livelihood was dependent upon seed. People's seed would produce crops that they could eat. They could also sell the harvest and obtain money for their everyday needs. Therefore, the number 5 has to do with God's provision for you.

The letter *hei* also means to be broken. It is often said that in order for one to truly give of oneself, one must be broken. This means that an individual is in a place of complete surrender and openness before God. In addition to brokenness, the number 5 represents revelation. Revelation is the making known of something that was previously hidden.

The body part given to this letter is the right foot. Anytime feet are mentioned in Scripture, it's symbolic of one's direction, destiny, ministry, or guidance. The right foot identifies a specific direction of authority. Authority is simply the power or right to do something.

By combining the information collected here, you can see how compacted the number 5 is. Remember that since Hebrew letters have a numerical value, the letters and numbers have associated meanings.

The Number 6

The Hebrew letter assigned to the number 6 is *vav*. This letter is associated with creation and the existence of humanity, and it further expresses God creating the earth. He declared "Let there be . . ." and there was (see Genesis 1). *Vav* emphasizes the phenomenon of light breaking forth through the darkness. The ray of light is said to be the secret of the letter *vav*. It deals with the external and internal force of creation.

The letter *vav* further reveals the hierarchical order within creation. This suggests that the number 6 is the number of humanity's creation. However, it also represents the order of creation. Furthermore, the number 6 could symbolize the reordering of an individual's life. In the natural creation, when the earth's components are out of order, disasters occur upon the earth. It's the exact same when it comes to people's lives. When our lives are out of order, it results in disaster. In that case, there is a need of reordering!

In the Hebrew, *vav* is referred to as *vav hachibur*. It's considered the *vav* of "connection." This information indicates that the number 6 represents connections. There is a type of connection I often refer to as a Kingdom connection. In other words, God has divinely orchestrated the paths of one individual to cross with the paths of another. The actual meaning of *vav* is a hook. A hook is often used in fishing. It's the hook on the rod that catches the fish. This is still symbolic of a connection. This is where we get the old phrase "hook up." The phrase means that an individual is connected with someone who can bring about benefits.

The body part given to *vav* is the right kidney. This is very interesting! You may be asking, "What does that mean?" In order to understand it completely, we must understand the function of the kidneys. The scientific function is to filter blood in order to excrete the unwanted waste products in urine. The kidneys also maintain the body's fluid and electrolytes at constant levels. That's a mouthful! In simple terms, the main component of the kidney is to filter the blood and get rid of unwanted waste. The number 6 therefore has to do with purifying the soul, spirit, and heart of a person. Jeremiah 17:9 informs us, "The heart is deceitful above all things, and desperately wicked; who can know it?" For this reason, there is a need for humankind to be purified and cleansed of wickedness and deceit.

The Number 7

In the Hebrew, *zayin* is the seventh letter of the *aleph-bet* and has the numeric value of 7. The pictograph of *zayin* looks like a sword, and the classical Hebrew script shows a *vav* with a large crown on its head. Therefore, *zayin* represents the crown or crowning of something.

The actual meaning of the word *zayin* is weapon or sword. However, it derives from the root word *zan*, meaning substance or nourishment, which is found in words like *mazon*, meaning food. How are food and nourishment connected to the sword? In the spiritual sense, in order to be at rest and nourished, we must sometimes engage in spiritual warfare.

Zayin represents the number 7 and a sword; therefore, it shouldn't be a surprise that this letter is used to cut up or divide time into units of seven. Some refer to it as the sword of time. The Jewish celebrate *Shabbat*, which is the seventh day of the seven-day week. They also celebrate *Shavu'ot*, which is the 49th day after Passover (the week of weeks). In addition, the Jewish celebrate *Shemitah*, which means that the seventh year is the year of rest for the land. The majority of the world today is run by the Gregorian calendar, which was implemented in 1582. This is the current calendar we use, but even on the Gregorian calendar there are seven days in a week. By this, we can clearly see that the number 7 represents periods or divisions of time.

In the Jewish tradition, the number 7 always represents the number of wholeness, completion, blessings, and rest. Furthermore, the body part assigned to this letter is the left foot. It represents motion and movement. Movement is a continual forward motion. It's a change or development of something or someone. The number 7 can therefore represent the completion of something that has been developed!

The Number 8

The letter assigned to the number 8 is *chet*, the letter of life. It represents the creative power of God. *Chet* (8) is also the number of grace and the number of wisdom. In addition to grace and wisdom, *chet* is the letter of light. It's said that *chet* represents that doorway to light from heaven. This is commonly known among the Jewish people as "run and return." It is the light that shines from God and is reflected back to Him from the soul. It runs and returns!

Chet is also the doorway of life. The letter resembles the doorway where the blood of the lamb was placed during the first Passover in Exodus 12:7. Furthermore, *chet* represents the concept of new beginnings. There are so many powerful examples of the number 8. Here are some examples:

- According to Jewish tradition, the covenant of circumcision occurs on the eighth day of a boy's life. This marks the beginning of his life.
- There were only eight souls who were saved during the Great Flood of Noah.
- David was the eighth son of Jesse.
- The Lord confirmed the validity of His covenant to Abraham eight times.

The body part assigned to the letter *chet* is the right hand. This represents a position of authority and government. The sense that is given to the letter *chet* is sight. Sight is your ability to see beyond where you are.

The Number 9

The Hebrew letter assigned to the number 9 is *tet*, which is also the first letter of the word *tov*, meaning good, in the Hebrew. Thus, this symbolizes hidden or inverted good. In other words, the good is hidden within! The secret of the letter *tet* is said to be the power of the mother to carry her concealed good (the baby) throughout the period of pregnancy. The number 9 therefore represents the power and ability to bring potential into actuality. It encompasses the revelation of birthing!

Although the letter *tet* represents hidden goodness, it can also represent goodness that has become perverted. It can represent impurity and filth. The body part that been assigned to the letter *tet* is therefore the left kidney, since a kidney purifies the blood and gets rid of unwanted waste. So the number 9 represents the purifying of that which is good. It's the ability to maintain the goodness within.

The physical sense given to the letter *tet* is hearing. This denotes that the number 9 represents your ability to hear in the Spirit. God is always speaking; however, mankind is not always in a position to hear what He is saying. This number urges you to listen carefully to the instructions of God.

The Number 10

The Hebrew letter assigned to the number 10 is *yud* (*yod*). The pictograph for the letter *yud* looks like an arm or hand. In fact, the body part assigned to the letter *yud* is the left hand. I believe the arm or hand here represents the divine help of God. This help can be seen as His supernatural provision.

Yud is the smallest of the Hebrew letters and is referred to as the "atom" of the consonants. It's the form from which all the other letters begin and end. In the Jewish tradition, it represents the divine point of energy. According to tradition, God uses the letters as the building blocks of creation. The letter *yud* therefore indicates God's omnipresence.

Yud is considered the starting point of all humanity. It's the spark of the Spirit of God. In Deuteronomy 7:7 (NLT), Israel is considered "the smallest of all nations." Within them, however, is the spark of God. Israel is considered a type of *yud*. All of this is encapsulated in the number 10.

The actual meaning of *yud* is the arm or hand, and the letter itself resembles a person in prayer. It suggests the hand or arm reaching toward heaven. This insinuates that the number 10 represents a spirit of prayer. Humankind is reaching up to God, and God is answering.

The number 10 also represents completion or order. For example, there were 10 things that God created on the first day, and 10 things He created at the end of the sixth day of creation. There were 10 generations from

Adam to Noah. The most evidential of God's order is that He gave us the Ten Commandments. In summation, the number 10 speaks of the divine order of God!

PROPHETIC INTEL

In the days ahead, God will begin to speak more and more through numbers, dates, and time frames. Don't think it's a strange thing to see repeating numbers or the same number stand out to you over a period of time. This may be God emphasizing the meaning behind that number. Some will think that this is you being too deep or "out there." But you are just prophetic. Embrace this part of who you are. God has always done everything in the Word in specific detail, with accurate counts of everything. The Bible says that He even knows the number of hairs on your head (see Luke 12:7). If God is so detailed as to have assigned numbers to the hairs on your head, how much more would He assign numerical value to the course of your life?!

Try the following prophetic activation to capture the numbers that are showing up in your life and process what they might mean to you.

- Write down which number or numbers you are seeing frequently (whether in dreams or in your everyday life).
- Search the Bible for Scriptures that contain these numbers. Write down what these verses mean to you.
- Search this chapter's text to see what the number or numbers you've listed mean in Hebrew. Note down how they apply to your life and to this current season you are in.
- Write a prayer or declaration for yourself connecting to the biblical meaning of the numbers God has emphasized to you.

PART TWO

A GLIMPSE INTO THE FUTURE

5

Alternate Timeline

The Days of Noah

And as it was in the days of Noah, so it will be also in the days of
the Son of Man . . .

Luke 17:26

The unique ministry God has given me the privilege to serve in has taken
me around the world. As a prophet, I've been invited to some of the most
interesting places on assignment. I was on a ministry tour of seven countries
a few years ago that landed me back in Geneva, Switzerland. I had been
there in 2018 and then again after the world was rocked by a pandemic. My
hosts were some of the most genuine, God-fearing believers I've ever met.

Switzerland is one of the most beautiful places I've ever been to. Imagine a popular vacation area, mixed with the finest luxury clothing and
jewelry, and the highest quality dining, all surrounded by the greenest
hills and valleys. It's the kind of place you want to retire to, or at least
vacation in frequently. On this trip, I saw hot-air balloons floating in the
distance on one side of the sky above. On the other side was an array of

colorful wings from several hang gliders that had dived off a cliff. The temperature that time of year was perfect. It was warm, with just the right breeze in the air.

I was there to meet with a group of leading prophets who were standing as the gatekeepers of their nation. When I arrived to meet these amazing people for the first time, one of them said, "We just watched you on TV, and now you're here!"

Another one continued, "Your words that you shared blessed us so much."

Someone else exclaimed, "We've been reading your book!"

I was puzzled. I wanted to know where they had seen me on TV in their country. I had been traveling for months and hadn't filmed for TV during that time. I found out that through the power of the media, the airing of an international show I had been on a year before was just now reaching their country. I thought to myself, *How cool is that? The message God had me share is literally traveling the globe. Thank you, Jesus!*

After adjusting to the area, I realized that there was no time to waste. I quickly rushed to my first assignment. We met for strategic, prophetic prayer at the United Nations. I had been invited to visit there before and had toured and met with key people to minister to them prophetically. This time, it was more of a gritty ministry journey. My team and I met with groups both outside and inside the facilities.

I happened to be in Geneva on the exact day that they were relaunching the Large Hadron Collider (LHC) in April 2022. It's the world's largest and most powerful particle accelerator. It's a device used to boost subatomic particles such as protons—accelerated to a speed close to the speed of light.[1] It's a mysterious project collaborated on by ten thousand of the world's top scientists. It's my understanding that their goal is to manipulate or experiment with dark matter, which is believed to be the foundation block for everything that we know of in the universe. Dark matter is the dominating form of energy in the cosmos.[2] It has been widely theorized that these scientists' goal is to pull things out of the invisible realm into our reality, and to manipulate space and time. As farfetched as it may sound, time travel and harnessing the power of the universe has been all the chatter among those connected to this project.

The Timeline Has Shifted

The LHC is housed at CERN, an acronym for the French name of the European Council for Nuclear Research. CERN is a controversial facility because many people believe that its logo is in the shape of 666. CERN is also historically significant because of what has been invented or discovered since its inception. In 1989, British scientist Tim Berners-Lee invented the World Wide Web (WWW) while working at CERN.[3] It was also the place where the Higgs boson particle was discovered,[4] among many other things.

My meeting just so happened to be at CERN. This was my second time there, but this time the relaunch of the LHC was causing such a hustle and bustle in the area. Locals told me that for months they were experiencing constant power outages, especially people who lived near the facility. In the midst of the meeting, prophecy began to stir up concerning the secret project that some heads of nations were engaging in. Whether or not scientists at CERN are attempting to create portals into alternate dimensions is debatable, but clearly there were diabolic plans going on that people were not being made fully aware of. I was also taken to the World Health Organization (WHO), and then the World Council of Churches (WCC) locations. While I was in conversations and meetings in these places, the Lord had me on a prophetic stealth assignment. I saw visions of what was about to be unveiled and the next major agendas that would shake the earth.

As I stood in my meeting at CERN, the Lord showed me something about the timeline we're on. I heard Him say, *The timeline has shifted.* The world we have come to know, and many have come to love, has drastically changed. God told me, *The days of Noah have returned.*

People in Noah's days were enjoying their lives as if nothing were happening around them. They were going on with life as usual, when the world as they knew it was ending. Matthew 24:37–39 (ESV) says this:

> For as were the days of Noah, so will be the coming of the Son of Man. For as in those days before the flood they were eating and drinking, marrying and giving in marriage, until the day when Noah entered the ark, and they were unaware until the flood came and swept them all away, so will be the coming of the Son of Man.

It's the same now, in our time—people are going about as if we've not come to the end of an era. They are going on as usual, as if there is no warning call being released throughout the world to come to Jesus Christ!

Parallels to the Days of Noah

What was going on in the days of Noah that parallels what we see in our own time, and what we will see in the years to come? A number of things were happening then that are also happening now: a population explosion, the widespread expansion of perversion, the distortion of gender and godly roles, brazen pride, a sharp increase of violence and lawlessness, and the manipulation of human DNA. Let's look at these parallels between our day and the days of Noah a little more closely.

A population explosion

Genesis 6:1 explains that during the time of Noah there was a population explosion on the earth. It marked a period of exponential multiplication. People came into a time where the birthrate far exceeded the death rate. Due to God's grace, many people were living long and healthy lives. Longer lives and an increasing population are characteristic of our day as well.

Widespread perversion

In the days of Noah, there was extreme sexual perversion. People operated in a spirit of lawlessness. There was nothing off-limits and no standard of integrity that they were willing to abide by. Genesis 6:5 (ESV) says, "The LORD saw that the wickedness of man was great in the earth, and that every intention of the thoughts of his heart was only evil continually." People developed wicked hearts as they began to turn away from God's principles and laws. This is very much like the widespread perversion we are seeing today, and unfortunately, it's becoming worse.

The distortion of gender and godly roles

With extreme perversion comes the distortion of gender roles, along with identity confusion. In Noah's day, people began to turn their affections to things that were unnatural, as well as placing the creation above the Creator. This was a reversal of order and godly roles. In Luke 17:22–30 (ESV), Jesus connects the days of Noah to the same wickedness and perversion that destroyed Sodom. He told His disciples,

> The days are coming when you will desire to see one of the days of the Son of Man, and you will not see it. And they will say to you, "Look, there!" or "Look, here!" Do not go out or follow them. For as the lightning flashes and lights up the sky from one side to the other, so will the Son of Man be in his day. But first he must suffer many things and be rejected by this generation. Just as it was in the days of Noah, so will it be in the days of the Son of Man. They were eating and drinking and marrying and being given in marriage, until the day when Noah entered the ark, and the flood came and destroyed them all. Likewise, just as it was in the days of Lot— they were eating and drinking, buying and selling, planting and building, but on the day when Lot went out from Sodom, fire and sulfur rained from heaven and destroyed them all—so will it be on the day when the Son of Man is revealed.

The wicked condition of the human heart in these times brought about every twisted, perverted, and unquenchable lustful desire. People felt justified in living to satisfy their desires. They felt as though they could live however they desired and no one had a right to judge them in their iniquity. They had the mindset that "if it feels good to you, then you can do whatever makes you happy." They redefined truth and made it an interpretation, an expression, or an experience rather than an absolute. Sound familiar?

Brazen pride

All of this was rooted in pride. People both in Noah's day and in the days of Sodom had a staunch, brazen unwillingness to admit the error of their ways. God is so merciful to us that He warns us in love and overextends to us grace, yet many still reject Him. People were so full of pride in those days that they refused to hear the truth and change their hearts. God is so wonderful and compassionate that He didn't destroy them for their sin.

What He allowed destruction to come upon them for was their refusal to change, their runaway pride.

The Bible lists three things that the people of Sodom's pride manifested in: "Behold, this was the guilt of your sister Sodom: she and her daughters had pride, excess of food, and prosperous ease, but did not aid the poor and needy" (Ezekiel 16:49 ESV). Let's examine this scenario more closely, which reveals even more parallels with our own days:

- *Excess of food*: The people of Sodom had so much food that one could argue that plenty and waste had become part of their culture. They could be viewed as a people who had everything, but still remained empty inside. I don't know about where you live, but I can definitely see the parallels to my country today. That's just like sin and the path of the enemy. The devil will promise you everything, but leave you empty.

- *Prosperous ease*: These people trusted in things, their wealth, and their resources. Their prosperity caused them to become idle, comfortable, and complacent. They lost their work ethic, and lost touch with what it means to put toil and effort into what you want to achieve. Because of this, they did the bare minimum. Likewise, we are seeing this in many Western countries today.

- *Neglecting the poor*: The poor are the ones who don't have enough money or resources to sustain themselves. Due to classism, life circumstances, widowhood, being abandoned as children, having a chronic disease or infirmity, or the like, the poor cannot support themselves. The days of Noah, linked here to the days of Sodom, show that it's highly possible that the people and government of those times did not properly care for the poor. The Bible says in several other translations of Ezekiel 16:49 that they did not "strengthen the hand of the poor." To strengthen the poor doesn't just mean to give them food, temporary shelter, or a little money. To strengthen them means to give them the necessary tools to create their own resources. A community, city, or nation neglecting their own poor is the highest sign of the brazen, stiff-necked pride that swells within it.

Increasing violence and lawlessness

Genesis 6:11 (ESV) says, "Now the earth was corrupt in God's sight, and the earth was filled with violence." That word *violence* is the Hebrew word *chamac*, meaning injustice, wrongdoing, and as mentioned, violence.[5] Violence is behavior intended to harm, damage, or even kill someone else. The level of destruction in the days of Noah was off the charts. The hearts of people were against one another. This caused a level of corruption that had never been seen until this time to spread among the masses.

As it was in the days of Noah, so it is today—that spirit of lawlessness is running throughout the earth. It is on display everywhere, being shown from the highest levels of government to the average person who lacks love.

The manipulation of human DNA

According to Genesis 6:2, the fallen beings that many refer to as fallen angels came and slept with the women of the earth, producing a hybrid race of species with superhuman strength and abilities. Today, we would call this transhumanism. It is the philosophy and movement that advocates for the enhancement of humanity and the human condition through technologies that can enhance the human experience. (We will discuss this further in chapter 7, where I talk about genetic recoding and the return of the Nephilim.)

A Beacon of Light in the Night

Are you seeing now how the timelines between Noah's days (and even Sodom's) and our own are just about identical? We are living in the days of Noah, or might as well be. Regardless of the year we are living in as you read this, the days of Noah are here.

The Church, and we as individual believers, cannot escape these days. Nor do we have the power to make other people adhere to the Word of God. But we can be an example of what it means to live out His Word, and we can let our love draw others to Him.

The return of Jesus Christ is closer than when we first believed. That's so exciting to think about! This means, however, that the world around us will grow more and more wicked as people's hearts wax colder and colder. This also means that we have a responsibility to evangelize, reach the lost, and be the hands and feet of Jesus in the earth. We can be a beacon of light, flickering in the deepest black of night.

PROPHETIC INTEL

The days of Noah have returned, but these are also the days of Elijah for believers. Elijah walked so closely with God that he partnered with Him to see His plans fulfilled in the world. He became a friend of God. You, too, have the opportunity to partner with the Holy Spirit and see great wonders and beautiful signs, even in the darkest days.

In spite of what goes on in the world, your job is to be prepared and equipped with the Word of God, and to dwell in the secret place with the Holy Spirit. Your mission is to demonstrate the message of the Gospel wherever you go. Our parallels to the days of Noah signify that a symbolic flood is coming. This time, however, it will be a flood of the glory of God covering the earth. Romans 5:20 states that "where sin abounded, grace abounded much more."

No matter how much sin or evil pervades these times, grace will always overshadow what is not of God. God is placing you in a spiritual ark of safety. Here are five components of this ark of God in our modern times:

Ark of Safety

1. God is stirring up communities of prayer that will raise a wall of protection and a hedge over His people. When the enemy releases a demonic attack, through prayer we will see the hand of the Lord intervene. Prayer will be one of the most needed spiritual weapons to combat darkness.

2. Because of the perilous and dangerous times, God will raise up safe havens throughout the nations. These will be Christian communities that understand the power of collaboration. These units of people will engage in group economics. They will come

together to store food in times of famine, buy buildings, farms, and houses to advance the Kingdom, become their own banks, and have all things in common, as we see among the believers in Acts 2:44.

3. Education centers will be developed that will infuse the next generation with a biblical foundation and advanced academics. You will see teachers, educators, and mentors who have a spiritual and prophetic burden to protect young people. These anointed people will be instrumental in seeing the Kingdom of God invade the education system. Schools, learning centers, and the like will be built that defend biblical values. This will be a huge component of God's ark of safety for the challenging days ahead.

4. Marriages and family units that reflect Christ and His Bride (the Church) will be restored and established. As in the days of Noah, the enemy will throw everything he can into tearing down the family unit and releasing a false identity and perversion, a twisting of God's original intent. But God is raising up a remnant of those who will take marriage and family back for the Kingdom of God.

5. Houses of glory will be erected. Many people will see and experience the glory of the Lord as lives are transformed by the power of Jesus. These places will be houses of worship (churches), but also individual homes that have become *bethel*, the place where the Spirit of God dwells.

6

A Crack in the White House Wall

For unto us a Child is born, unto us a Son is given; and the government
will be upon His shoulder.

Isaiah 9:6

I was picked up in a black government vehicle that I didn't know was coming. It was early morning. You could still see the blackness of the dawn. I
can still see the empty street in my mind, just blocks away from the White
House. I thought at the time, *This is odd. There's always movement in this
part of the District.*

I got this eerie feeling. I had my assistant ask who had sent for this car.
The car's occupants knew the specific details of where I would be headed,
and it seemed they knew who I was. The car was unmarked. Days before,
I had just come from releasing the word of the Lord in Washington, DC,
and visiting the White House. Earlier, a government official had told me,
"If you see . . . [this type of] vehicle, then it's the CIA or FBI."

I was unbothered by that, since I thought something like this could never
happen to me. I've only seen such things in movies. After all, I'm just a
preacher. I love my country and pray for it often.

Nervous and unsure when the vehicle pulled up, I still felt I had to get in. Once inside, I was questioned about where I had just been and what I had done. I answered truthfully.

A Prophetic Mission and Meeting

Okay, let's back up! Let's rewind to the events that occurred before this. I had been invited to Washington, DC, for a meeting and what I call a prophetic mission. I felt an urgency to go. As I prayed about it, the Holy Spirit spoke to me and commissioned me on this assignment. Whenever I experience this kind of urgency, it becomes top priority at that moment. I dropped everything to prepare for this. I was going to meet with a group of people to minister to them.

In addition, I was invited to come to the White House. What an amazing honor this was to have the privilege of standing on the very grounds where the forefathers of this nation had stood, and to walk the very halls and corridors that my ancestors had built with their bare hands and the sweat of their brow. Although the government itself didn't own slaves in 1792, it did turn to African Americans, both those who were enslaved and those who were free, to provide the majority of the labor that built the White House, United States Capitol, and other government buildings. I felt a sense of connection as I marveled at the sheer grit, workmanship, and architectural prowess of my people.

During the Christmas holidays, the time of year when I made this trip, the White House was decorated beautifully. Everywhere you looked, there were trees decorated in opulence. The lavish greenery, radiating gold and silver, mixed tastefully with shades of red. You could tell every detail had been thought out and meticulously organized. It was pure elegance in this vintage house representing the strength of our country. It stands there as a beacon of light. There's something quite special about it. If you've ever been to the White House, then you know it's actually much smaller than you'd picture it in your mind. Yet somehow, as I stood in the entrance, it felt humongous, and I felt so tiny. I thought to myself, *God why do you have me here?* I felt a bit inadequate for whatever I was going to do.

Just before my visit, the Holy Spirit had told me to anoint the bottom of my shoes with anointing oil as I walked the grounds, and to anoint myself to be consecrated. In the course of this visit, I would meet several key people who would need my prayer and ministry. The Spirit said to me, *A great transition is coming in the nation, and intercessors are needed to pray and release the word of the Lord. At this time, I've called you as a transitional prophet to stand in the gap for the nation and the people.*

Vision of a Fracturing Foundation

I was at the White House for hours, staying for a party convening later that evening. I met people in government and other industries. The Lord gave me an unusual vision. While the people were laughing and enjoying the festive time of year, I had this uneasy sense come over me. I had already had the opportunity to pray with a group of people and prophesy concerning the government. But in the midst of the evening's celebration, I felt sorrow, as if my spirit was weeping. Later in this vision, the White House walls inside became very visible. It's as if they stood out. I could see the most striking meandering fracture spreading in the wall, going all the way down to the floor. I heard the words *"a crack in the wall of the White House."*

What did this mean? I wondered. *Why would God show me a crack in the wall of the most powerful house in the world?*

This crack in the White House wall was symbolic of a fracture in the foundation of the nation. I saw it spreading, and I perceived that the crack is due to the moral decay, corruption, wickedness, and idolatry. People have turned away from serving God. Many leaders within government, and some leaders within the Church, have turned against the ways and principles of the Most High God.

Seven Fracture Points/Seven Healing Acts

The Lord allowed me to know that the fracture in the wall going down to the foundation represents a divide and separation from truth, a drifting from the principles of the Word of God. Only repentance, prayer, and turning back to the heart of God can mend the fracture, which started small but began to grow before my eyes.

There are seven of what I call "fracture points," which have the ability to stagnate a nation, a city, a community, a family, or even an individual. They are:

1. Idolatry
2. Perversion
3. Deceit
4. Dishonor
5. Rebellion
6. False religion
7. Breaking of God's laws

You may be reading this and living in another country outside the United States. This word isn't relegated to America. It's the same for your nation. These fracture points are occurring in so many places in our day. Yet if we pray, repent, humble ourselves, and seek the face of God, we can see our cities and nations heal, prosper, and follow the plan of God.

Jeremiah 29:7 (NIV) tells us, "Seek the peace and prosperity of the city to which I have carried you into exile. Pray to the LORD for it, because if it prospers, you too will prosper." It's imperative that you as a believer pray for the peace and prosperity of your city or nation. Your personal prosperity is in ways tied to it. If your country's government or economy fails, your own economy and quality of life will be negatively impacted. It's impossible to live in a nation and not somehow be even narrowly impacted by what happens to that nation.

We will talk more in chapter 8, "Superstorms," about how Elijah prophesied a drought in his region. He was also affected by that same drought. Although he was the very prophet who gave the word, he was not exempt from having to change his quality of life because of it. God gave him instructions to go to the Brook Cherith, where he would be fed by ravens and could drink. Likewise, no matter what happens to your city, community, or nation, God is faithful to guide His people. It is within your best interests, however, to seek the peace and prosperity of wherever you reside so that you, too, may prosper.

Here are seven acts that will heal a fracture in a nation, city, community, or individual:

1. Repentance
2. Heartfelt prayer
3. Fasting
4. Honor
5. True surrender to God
6. Being a solution
7. Keeping covenant with God

Key Prophecies in DC

In the prophetic meeting I mentioned having while on this assignment in Washington, DC, the Lord said several key things to me that we would see in the coming years. Let's look at a few of these key prophetic words.

The House of Saul will rise and fall

There will be a shake-up, a great shift within the United States government, as well as governments around the world. Just like during the time of ancient Israel, people will have to choose whether they will have leaders like Saul or leaders like David. Although Saul was anointed by the prophet Samuel, he was also a ruler the people elected based on his stature, outward appearance, and their fleshly desire to have Israel be like other nations (see 1 Samuel 10:17–24). Governments around the world will begin to choose if they want to go in the way of Saul.

Saul represents a mixture. In 1 Samuel 15, Saul disobeyed God's command when God told him to destroy the Amalekites and all their animals. The Lord therefore rejected Saul as king over Israel because he placed his personal, fleshly desires above the will of the Lord. In our day, Saul-type systems and governments will appear to rise for a period in the earth, but they are crumbling infrastructures that will become sepulchers for those leaders who are ruling but are spiritually dead.

There is a modern-day battle going on between the house of Saul and the house of David—representing two styles of leaders, two types of systems, and two ways of governing people. This clash will also appear within the leadership of the Church. God is not looking for dictators, He is looking to use those who are servant leaders. These are people who love God with all their hearts and love His people. Many Saul-like ministries will diminish, although they will appear to swell for a season. It's important to remember that all swelling is not growth or increase. Some swelling is due to infection and will soon burst.

Leaders like David will begin to rise

"Now there was a long war between the house of Saul and the house of David. But David grew stronger and stronger, and the house of Saul grew weaker and weaker" (2 Samuel 3:1). David-like leaders will begin to rise. David had a heart after God, according to 1 Samuel 13:14. He did not originally have the appearance of a great leader. He was simply a shepherd boy, a psalmist, a sensitive worshiper—but one who would soon become a mighty warrior. Davidic leaders know how to balance art and war, brute force and gentle care. They lead with soft power.

In the coming days, the Church will be like the house of David. These types of systems will grow stronger and help steer the direction of nations. The Church will no longer look to government, presidents, or congressmen or congresswomen for direction. These are all flawed and will never live up to the standard that only God can bring.

Corrupt politics that has invaded, torn apart, and caused great division within the Church has begun to stink in the nostrils of God. I strongly believe He has grown tired of the infighting over candidates and political parties. The Kingdom of God is so much bigger than a political party or candidate. Have we forgotten that no matter who is in power, believers have the ability to legislate God's will in the earth from our positions of spiritual authority?

You are a David-like leader whom God is raising up to effect change, shift atmospheres, bring conviction about wrongdoing, and demonstrate the love of Jesus Christ. This is not predicated on your title, position, or resume. God is choosing you because you have a heart after Him. He is choosing you because of His own pleasure.

Prophecy of a coming civil war

America and the nations will go through many changes, the Lord said to me. *At times in the near future, America will look like a third-world nation. You will not recognize your own country.*

There will be a great clashing that occurs, and pandemonium in the streets. Some will amass weapons and take up arms to fight against their neighbor. Many will be deceived into thinking that this is the way to protect and defend their country. In the vision from God, I saw bloodshed and civil unrest. There was such a huge commotion as buildings were being set on fire because of the political upheaval. People will not like the direction this nation is going, and an unprecedented shift will occur in the highest seat of the land. At that time, the National Guard will be called in, and people in troublesome areas will be placed under strict curfews and governance. This will only fan the flames.

During this time, the Church will have to increase her prayer. Strategic intercessors will arise to pour oil in the wounds of the land.

The Rest of the Story

To finish the odd story I started this chapter with, after delivering the key prophetic words in the nation's capital that I just related to you, I was picked up by that black vehicle and driven to a specific location. At first, I didn't realize that I was being interrogated. But then question followed question in rapid succession. I was asked about the reason I had come to DC, what I was doing in the area, and why I was doing it.

These initial questions led to even more questions. I was in shock because the whole experience felt like being in a movie. *I'm just a preacher doing the work of ministry*, I thought to myself. *This is so unnecessary.*

It all happened so fast, and later I tried to explain it away or make sense of it. I decided to share what had happened to me with my contacts in government, and they assured me it was indeed our government intelligence agencies behind that interesting scenario.

| PROPHETIC INTEL |

Over the next several months and years, governments will be shaken to their core. Nations and individual people will have the option to choose the way of the Lord or the evil pursuits of their hearts. Yes, we will see goat and sheep governments and nations—meaning they will be either rebellious or God-fearing. Seven governmental shifts are coming among the nations:

1. A shift is coming to political and governmental leaders. God will begin to judge those who have corrupt hearts. Those who operate as Saul did will become weaker in their influence and reach. Those who operate like David will rise and come into prominence.

2. A shift is coming to the legal system. There will be a fierce battle over key laws yet again. The Supreme Court will try unprecedented cases that change the landscape of America. Western nations will have to come to terms with what we believe and the direction we will go in.

3. A shift is coming in power structures and influence. Structures and organizations that have not defended the poor and underprivileged will be severely shaken by the hand of the Lord. The heart of God is to defend those who cannot defend themselves.

4. A shift is coming politically with young people. There will be a clashing of ideologies and values. Out of the clashing, a remnant of young adults, teenagers, and children will rise with a voice like a trumpet. That remnant will stand for biblical values. They will be the voice of the future!

5. A shift is coming over spiritual and natural wombs. You will see a curse broken off the next generation. Mothers will be carrying the

next generation's leaders, prophets, and government officials who are going to rule righteously.

6. A shift is coming to the order, ranking, and placement of nations. Some countries that have been at the top as far as production, manufacturing, economics, and technology will see a decline as there is a balancing of scales. Other nations that have been oppressed and riddled with challenges and struggles will see a status change as their people who love God are praying. Such believers will also see a status change. Some nations will advance in order to fulfill biblical prophecy.

7. A shift is coming to mindsets. Repentance will be the key that unlocks the Kingdom and power of God. No matter the city, region, or country that you live in, when you accept Jesus, you then become a part of the government of God. Your mind will be transformed to walk in the transformative power of Jesus Christ.

7

Genetic Recoding

Return of the Nephilim

For the life of the flesh is in the blood, and I have given it for you on the altar to make atonement for your souls, for it is the blood that makes atonement by the life.

Leviticus 17:11 ESV

We are at the turn of an age. It is a time when we go from one world system to another world system. Every time humanity enters a transition period like this, there is a great harvest of souls. Some leave this earthly life and transition to the next. But some are given divine instructions on how not only to navigate the transition, but also to build spiritual arks so that their families and loved ones are saved as well. Noah is an archetype of transitioning in the turn of an age. But rather than looking at his strategy, we will be focusing on what was taking place on the earth in his time and how it applies to us today.

In the days leading up to Noah's time, people were multiplying and having children, and daughters were being born to them. Angels who were called "the sons of God" in Genesis 6:2, but who were actually fallen angels, saw that these human daughters were fair, so they took them for themselves as wives, to mate with them. The resulting offspring were called "mighty men," and some were also "giants" on the earth in those days:

> Now it came to pass, when men began to multiply on the face of the earth, and daughters were born to them, that *the sons of God saw the daughters of men,* that they were beautiful; and they took wives for themselves of all whom they chose.
>
> And the LORD said, "My Spirit shall not strive with man forever, for he is indeed flesh; yet his days shall be one hundred and twenty years." There were *giants on the earth* in those days, and also afterward, when the sons of God came in to the daughters of men and they bore children to them. Those were *the mighty men* who were of old, men of renown.
>
> Then the LORD saw that the wickedness of man was great in the earth, and that every intent of the thoughts of his heart was only evil continually. And the LORD was sorry that He had made man on the earth, and He was grieved in His heart. So the LORD said, "I will destroy man whom I have created from the face of the earth, both man and beast, creeping thing and birds of the air, for I am sorry that I have made them." But Noah found grace in the eyes of the LORD.
>
> This is the genealogy of Noah. Noah was a just man, perfect in his generations. Noah walked with God. And Noah begot three sons: Shem, Ham, and Japheth.
>
> Genesis 6:1–10, emphasis added

The word *giant* in this passage is the Hebrew word *nphiyl,* or in English Nephilim.[1] The offspring of the fallen angels and daughters of men don't appear to all have had the same characteristics. Some were giants, while some were just mighty or valiant men known for their abnormal strength, their abilities as warriors, and their skill at completing remarkable feats. Deuteronomy 2 tells us that there were groups of giants called by different names. Not only were there the Anakim (the descendants of Anak), but some others were called the Emim, the Rephaim, and the Zamzummim. Although the words used to describe the offspring differ, the descriptors are the same. For instance, one of the definitions for *giants* was "the fallen." The angels were also called the fallen angels. One of the definitions for the word *offspring* was "giant." These offspring had unusual height and were also remarked to be tyrants.

The story doesn't end there, however. God repented of making humans on the earth because the hearts and thoughts of humankind were so evil. He decided to destroy the earth with a flood. Yet God sees that Noah is perfect. (The Bible says he was perfect.) This doesn't mean that Noah didn't make any mistakes. It means that he was pure, and his DNA was pure. He didn't have any defect. So by saving Noah's family, God started the process of cleansing human DNA from any mixture with fallen angels and giants. It was always God's desire to protect the DNA He had placed into humankind. Satan, on the other hand, always desires to corrupt the DNA.

We are given divine DNA, as well as the biological form. I call it a blood transfusion from Christ's redemptive work on the cross. His blood was shed for the remission of our sins and has the transformative power to change us, even to this day. The power of the blood of Jesus has transformed our spiritual DNA. When we receive Jesus, He restores us to His original plan in Genesis, where it tells us we were made in the image and likeness of God. This means God placed His glory in us. I believe that running through our veins is an infusion of the glory of God. Look at 2 Corinthians 3:18, in two different translations:

> "But we all, with open face beholding as in a glass the glory of the Lord, are changed into the same image from glory to glory, even as by the Spirit of the Lord" (KJV).

> "And all of us, as with unveiled face, [because we] continued to behold [in the Word of God] as in a mirror the glory of the Lord, are constantly being transfigured into His very own image in ever increasing splendor and from one degree of glory to another; [for this comes] from the Lord [Who is] the Spirit" (AMPC).

The word here for glory is *doxa*, and it means magnificence, excellence, dignity, and grace.[2] The word *transfigure* here means to transform into something more beautiful or elevated. So, our divine DNA is the image of God that we were created with in Genesis 1:26.

The Enemy Is after the Blood

DNA is a nucleic acid that carries the genetic information in the cell and is capable of self-replication and the synthesis of RNA. DNA consists of two long chains of nucleotides twisted into a double helix and joined by hydrogen bonds between the complementary bases adenine and thymine, or cytosine and guanine. The sequence of nucleotides determines individual hereditary characteristics. We call it our bloodline. Leviticus 17:11 says that the life of the flesh is in the blood. Blood is the flow and source of life. It is the real battlefield of the enemy. Whenever he wants to attack a family, he targets the bloodline by creating patterns and cycles of abuse, destructive thinking, or sickness that are passed down from generation to generation. When the enemy wants to influence people to cause them to be born with desires, beliefs, or human behaviors that are against the Word of God, he targets the blood.

In the New Testament, when Herod the Great, king of Judea, knew by way of the astrologers that the Messiah would be born, he ordered the execution of all the male children in Bethlehem and the surrounding region. When the devil wanted to stop God from coming through the human bloodline, he influenced evil men to kill the next generation. The enemy knows that when God moves, He comes through the blood because that's the way God set the universal laws to operate. No human being and nothing of significance that affects humankind can come to the earth except through a womb.

When God releases healing to a family, He changes one person and positively affects the bloodline. When God wants to raise up a generation of believers, He starts with one person and replicates that in his or her seed. But you see, anything that the enemy does, he takes it from God's idea and perverts or twists it.

Another Species in the Earth

In Numbers 13:33, we are at a place in history after the flood. The children of Israel sent a dozen spies out into the Promised Land. Ten of the twelve spies returned with a bad report, saying that there were giants in the land: "There we saw the giants (the descendants of Anak came from the giants); and we were like grasshoppers in our own sight, and so we were in their sight."

The giants are described here as being the sons or Anak (`*Anaq* in Hebrew[3]) which come from the giants (*Nephil*), the Nephilim. This goes all the way back to Genesis 6, when the fallen angels came and slept with human women. Satan tampered with the human DNA and created a hybrid race, part human and part angel or supernatural being. This was Satan's strategy back then to manipulate the blood, and he's still tampering with human bloodlines today, as we will talk about in a moment.

When the children of Israel were on their way out of the wilderness, we read about what Deuteronomy 2:10–11 refers to as Rephaim. They are called Emims by the Moabites, a giant breed described as being as tall as the Anakims. The root word for their name means terrors. They, like the other giant breeds, were problematic for those who didn't have the DNA mixture or who were not subjugated to them.

Deuteronomy 2:20 describes a land of the giants in Ammon where the Zamzummims lived. They, like the Emims, were many and also as tall as the Anakims, but according to verse 21, the Lord destroyed them before the children of Israel arrived to pass through that land. God has the children of Israel continue to purify the land from the giants. They got to a point where in that region, only the king of Og was left of the giants. He was so large that his bed measured 9 cubits long by 4 cubits wide, which is an estimated 13.5 feet high and 6 feet wide. It was also made of iron instead of wood.

As we progress further into the conquest of the Promised Land, however, you see that the children of Israel didn't fully vanquish all the giants. The Israelites ended up in a tense standoff with the Philistine army, and there was a mighty man who was a giant taunting their army and defying the name of Yahweh. We all know the story of David and Goliath (see 1 Samuel 17). After David defeated Goliath, he and his servants went on to defeat several other giants of the Rephaim race. Some were characterized as having deformities, such as six fingers and toes on each hand and foot.

It was easy for the children of Israel to defeat the giants once they believed they could do it—and once they stopped viewing themselves as grasshoppers. The mighty men who could do amazing feats were sometimes a different story. They often were revered by their own people and rose to positions of power and influence, yet they weren't always easy to spot because they physically looked the same as regular people.

Whenever we discuss giants, the most obvious question is, "How did the giants survive the Flood?" Many scholars agree that God stated that the flood would destroy life *on the face of the earth*. They believe that these giants, and possibly some of the mighty men, had the knowledge to live underground, and that some of them survived the storm. It isn't totally clear how they reemerged after the Flood. What is clear is that giants are mentioned numerous times in the Bible. There appear to have been several races of giants that occupied large territories and oppressed non-giant races. It was never God's will for humankind to distort and mix our DNA. Each person is a unique design, a reflection of the Father. And when we accept Christ, as we walk in the Spirit we are being transformed from glory to glory into the image of Jesus Christ.

I'd like to finish this chapter on genetic recoding by sharing two prophecies with you.

Prophecy of the Nephilim's return

The world will see an unveiling of unusual sightings in the days ahead. People will call what they see aliens or extraterrestrials, but these will be ancient beings that have traversed the earth and skies for many eons. They are what we know as fallen angels or demons, and even a hybrid that has the ability to shape-shift into the appearance of a man or woman.

The masses will be puzzled at these sightings, but many governments around the world will be aware of the increase and will secretly withhold their findings. Because of where we are on the biblical timeline, these unexplained sightings will become more and more frequent. Some will call you crazy for even uttering it, but the Bible shows these beings' source of origin—the spirit realm. This earthly world, although physical, is powered by an invisible, unseen world. In order to fully understand what's happening, you must understand the spiritual world.

Just like in the Old Testament, this hybrid race will have advanced weapons and technology beyond human capability. In the days ahead, there will be sightings of objects, crafts, and other forms of technology that do not come from human hands or minds. As believers we are not to be alarmed, but are to be aware that there is much spiritual activity taking place in the heavenlies.

Cloning and genetic tampering prophecy

This may sound crazy to you as you read this, but God showed me a vision of a company based in Switzerland, and another in the United States, with cloning facilities. I could see that they had begun cloning animals. They were experimenting with bringing back animals that had become extinct. Although deemed illegal, they had also been experimenting with cloning people. I could see this contraption or technology that was created to mimic the womb of a woman. The scientists were so advanced that they could genetically engineer the race of an individual person, down to the eye color, hair color, and other physical features.

The Lord said to me, *These projects are being secretly conducted around the world. These people with wicked hearts seek to usurp My power by tampering with human life outside of My will. In the future, they will endeavor to make this an acceptable part of society. They will say, "We can create life." They will say, "We are gods." But their plans will be corrupt, and defects will emerge that will cause major concern.*

When God said this to me and showed me these things, I was completely in shock. What I saw appeared to be happening at this time, behind closed doors. It is a battle over the DNA of the earth's creatures—and over the future of the human bloodline. But the blood of Jesus has already prevailed against it.

| PROPHETIC INTEL |

The enemy has been after the blood, because he knows that there is life and value in the blood. For this reason, Christ shed His blood for you and me, so we could be free, delivered, saved, and completely transformed. We will see many diabolical things happening with human and animal

DNA in the future, from genetic modifications to cloning, and more. As a believer, however, you have an advantage. Because the precious blood of Jesus is applied to your life, you have access to God's supernatural power and covering. The blood of Jesus holds all power over the enemy and his evil schemes. Here are eleven attributes of the blood of Jesus Christ:

1. The blood of Jesus takes away our sin (see 1 John 1:7).
2. The blood of Jesus cleanses our minds from acts that lead to destruction (see Hebrews 9:14).
3. The blood of Jesus restores and redeems us (see Ephesians 1:7).
4. The blood of Jesus gives us peace and reconciles us back to our heavenly Father (see Colossians 1:20).
5. The shed blood of Jesus is the price paid so that we can have freedom (see Revelation 1:5).
6. The blood of Jesus will cause us to triumph over the enemy (see Revelation 12:11).
7. The blood of Jesus justifies us (puts us in right standing with God) and saves us from wrath (see Romans 5:9).
8. The blood of Jesus has broken us free from the curse of the Law and any generational curse in our family bloodline (see Galatians 3:13).
9. Because we are washed in the blood of Jesus, Jesus Christ testifies on our behalf that we have been cleansed (see Revelation 1:5).
10. Because of the blood of Jesus, we can be healed of sickness and disease (see Isaiah 53:5).
11. Because of the blood of Jesus, we are protected from evil, destruction, and harm (see Exodus 12:27).

8

Superstorms

But the weather changed abruptly, and a wind of typhoon strength (called a "northeaster") burst across the island and blew us out to sea.

Acts 27:14 NLT

I have always been fascinated with weather. I grew up in Florida, where it is basically a tropical rainforest. We had beautiful sunshine, warm weather, and the most amazing beaches. That could all change at the drop of a dime, and it would look as if you were driving through a monsoon. Beautiful days could quickly become covered with hurricane-force winds. This is nothing new to you, if you live in an area like I did.

When my family and I moved to North Carolina, it seemed like a different world to me. I had visited family there on many holidays, but to officially live there was exciting, scary, and bittersweet. So many in our family lived in Florida, and they were a huge part of our everyday life. I was just a child in elementary school, so you can imagine how enormous a change this was for me when we left.

One of the things I became highly fascinated with was the weather and environment in Raleigh, North Carolina. Florida was almost always hot; we never got even a flake of snow. I had seen snow in movies and seen pictures of it in books, but had never seen any in person. I was extremely excited to play in the snow. The first couple of years in the new city, however, there was no significant snowfall. Yet it just so happened that I had been reading about the prophet Elijah and how he seemed to have some ability to command the elements and they would obey. Although I was very young, I had been in ministerial training and a school of the prophets, and I had developed a close relationship with the Lord. I would teach at events for young people and minister to adults alike. More than those things, I had what was most valuable to me—a real relationship with the Holy Spirit. He was and is my best friend. That sounds odd to some people because they view the Holy Spirit as an *it* or a *thing* that comes on them, rather than as a precious, most valuable Person who lives in them. I learned early on that He is my everything and He will always be there for me.

At a young age I would prophesy, have prophetic dreams, and see visions that would come to pass. I didn't fully understand it all, but my parents and other ministers helped me understand what the Lord was showing me. I might have a vision of someone's death before it occurred unexpectedly or a vision of a baby's birth. I prophesied about so many children to the parents, when the parents had not even shared yet that they were pregnant. Sometimes the Lord would even give me the name and details about a child, which the parents had not shared with anyone. Once the child was born and had begun to grow, the parents would confirm everything the Lord had said to me.

I had come to the realization that because we weren't getting much snow in Raleigh initially, I had to create it. I know that sounds bizarre, but my mindset as a young prophet was that God has given us authority over the elements. I still believe that, to this day. My parents and the ministers who knew me then still tell a snow story about me. It was January 24, 2000. I only know this because there are news articles that still exist online about a storm that day. I had decided that I wanted to see blizzard-like snow. The meteorologists had determined that we wouldn't even get an inch. I ran to our back deck and began to prophesy to the sky, commanding the snow to come. My three brothers and parents watched as this happened. *There's Josh going out and prophesying to the sky. He's commanding the snow to come*, they thought.

I had never done anything like this and had never seen anyone do it, but I thought, *God is with me, so why not?* I laugh at the thought of this now. Maybe I could have prophesied about something else that would have improved our community, but the mind of a child is interesting. Snow is what I wanted, and I went for it. Childlike faith is so valuable. You believe God says you can have it, you believe Him for it, you decree His word, and then you prepare, plan, and wait for the manifestation.

All that evening, I kept going outside and prophesying to the sky, and then I would run back inside to check the weather report on TV. Overhead, I could see the clouds moving rapidly. As the clouds began to encircle us, it looked like being in the eye of a hurricane. I had faith that the sky was listening to me. The meteorologists on every major news channel said that this wouldn't be anything significant. I was determined that it would be. Finally, I had a breakthrough. The meteorologist said, "Wow, the snowfall amount just went up. It looks as if we will now be getting two inches."

That was a long way from the few centimeters' dusting of snow that they were previously predicting. But of course, I wasn't satisfied! In the Spirit, I saw more. So I ran back outside, and by then it was twilight. I looked up to the sky and said again, "I command the atmosphere to produce record-breaking snowfall. We will not just see a few inches. Clouds, you will release snow until I tell you to stop."

Next, the meteorologist on TV showed this seemingly little storm system. It was small and insignificant. Then he gave an update: "We don't know what just happened, but it seems as if we may actually get four or five inches."

I was grinning from ear to ear. *That's still not enough,* I thought. I ran back outside and began to speak loudly to the sky and atmosphere that the snowfall levels would increase again.

My neighbors had to think I was nuts, and maybe so did my brothers . . . or were they just used to me being a peculiar prophetic kid? I never really thought about how I looked. I just prayed. It was nearing my bedtime, and I had to attend my elementary school the next day. Of course, I typically had a curfew, but I boldly told my parents, "I'm not going to school tomorrow because it's going to snow."

I continued prophesying outside and checking the news inside. Late that night, the weatherman said, "It now looks as if we're going to get about six to eight inches." He continued, "We don't know what happened, but the storm is changing right in front of our eyes. All of our weather models were completely off." He looked again, and the predictions were now showing a foot of snow. He concluded wryly, "I'm just going to stop predicting the accumulation tonight. We don't know what might happen with this storm system!"

My family and I were laughing hysterically with excitement. They told me, "You prophesied this, and it's baffling the meteorologists!"

I knew for sure I would get a day off school. This snowstorm set a record in the area as the most snowfall accumulation in the history of Raleigh ever. It hasn't been broken since. We got over 24 inches of snow, and in some areas even more. It snowed and didn't stop for two days. We were out of school for over a week. The city couldn't operate, and roads couldn't be driven on. The storm became so massive that it spanned up and down the Eastern Seaboard. This had never happened before in our city, so the officials didn't know what to do.

The Lord used this situation to teach me never to lose faith even if others think you're crazy, and that if we partner with Him, we can speak to the elements and they obey.

Artificial Weather Systems

Weather is going to become more and more destructive in our world. It will become more noticeable as massive superstorms, tornadoes, hurricanes, tsunamis, monsoons, and the like sweep through the earth.

Some of these encounters with unprecedented weather will be because of the world's volatility. People's actions will affect nature. Even wickedness, lawlessness, and corruption will cause the earth to respond. Some of these unusual weather disruptions will be signs of God's judgment and cleansing in the earth.

Further, the Lord has begun to speak to me in detail concerning some unusual weather we will see in the coming days. I want to share with you what He has shown me about artificial weather systems that are even now under construction and being used.

Artificial weather systems will wreak havoc

The Lord showed me that artificial weather systems are being created and used by governments and nations around the world. In the realm of the spirit, I could see these manmade machines. Some were sitting out in and even under the ocean, far away from people. These technologically advanced systems have the ability to produce hurricanes and powerful storms that could spawn tornadoes, monsoons, and the like.

The Lord then showed me unnatural cloud cover. What I saw looked just like clouds and worked just like clouds, but they were not generated by natural means. They were produced or manufactured through cloud seeding and other forms of weather technology that have not been publicly revealed to the masses.

These artificial weather systems will begin to wreak havoc in the earth. Wicked men and women in high places will seek to use them to destroy and reconstruct cities and communities. They will also be used to exact methods of control and governance over certain areas. To justify their actions, these people will say, "We're helping the environment. We're bringing rain to areas that desperately need it. We're providing water for crops." Yet their real agenda will be far worse.

The Lord said to me that these people will begin to experiment with the sun. They are studying it so closely already to see if they can duplicate its effects and even block out the components of it that they don't want. This will prove disastrous. They cannot play as though they are God. There is only one God, and His creation and ability to govern our world cannot be mimicked, mocked, or duplicated.

Commanding the Elements

Thousands of years before us, the prophets of old were given the authority and power to command the elements, and the elements obeyed. Earth, water, air, and fire are regarded as the fundamental constituents of the world. It is these elements that govern the earth. The Greek word for element is *stoikheion*, which means step or component part.[1] It is these elemental components that help make up the world and help sustain life on earth. Within each element is an enormous amount of energy and power. Although the elements govern the earth, they were never meant to govern humanity. The Scriptures clearly state in Genesis 1 that God gave humankind dominion over the earth. That encompasses every component making up the earth.

God never created the elements to rule and govern humanity. Most people today, however, feel as though we have no control over what the elements do or don't do. The meaning of the word *govern* is to control, influence, or regulate.[2] Take a minute to analyze the elements' position on earth. In my analysis, I find that to some degree the elements do control, influence, and regulate the earth. However, God said that *we* were given dominance over the earth. This means we have authority over the elemental influences. The word *dominion* means to control. It comes from the Latin word *dominus*, which means lord or master.[3] That's simply an individual who is in charge. When you understand your God-given position of authority, you will then understand what it really means to command the elements.

In fact, what does it really mean to command? In the Bible, the word *command* is used over 100 times. In most cases, it refers to God and/or an individual commanding something or someone. In order to command something by God, an individual must first have God's approval and authority. The Hebrew definition of *command* comes from the word *tsavah*.[4] It means to charge, give orders, commission, and appoint. I believe that commanding is a vital part of life on earth. The entire world is run by a complex system of commands. Just think about it for a minute—the way we function as a human race has always been by commands.

Observe the system that governs our traffic, for instance. As you drive, various road signs tell you what to do. The signs tell you when to stop, yield, merge, and so forth. Why? Because people are not responsible enough to take these actions safely without the enforcement of the law. If the signs weren't there, most drivers wouldn't take the necessary actions. As it is in the natural, so it is in the spiritual. The spirit world is also governed by a system of commands. It goes all the way back to the beginning of time, when God spoke "Let there be . . ." Because we are made in the image of God, we the righteous have been given commanding power!

Atmospheric Phenomena

For too long, the elements earth, water, air, and fire have dictated to us how it will be. Because the sons and daughters of God have not been in their rightful place, the Spirit of God has allowed the elements to send us messages. The earth continues to send its quakes. The air continues to spin tornadoes and whirlwinds. Fires continue to burn rapidly and uncontrollably. Waters have flooded, and in many areas rain has been withheld. What are the elements trying to tell us? Through these common occurrences or atmospheric phenomena, the elements speak of the changing times.

First Chronicles 12:32 says, "Of the sons of Issachar who had understanding of the times, to know what Israel ought to do, their chiefs were two hundred; and all their brethren were at their command." This Scripture explains that the sons of Issachar had something special. They had the ability to discern the spiritual times and seasons. Because they had an understanding of the times, they had instructions for Israel. They knew what Israel was supposed to do. Furthermore, the latter part of this verse reveals something so phenomenal—it says that their brethren were at the chiefs' or leaders' command. I believe this introduces a prophetic principle to the Body of Christ: In order to command, one must have the divine (God-given) ability to discern the times and seasons.

Because there haven't been many righteous prophets and prophetic people to proclaim the direction of the Body of Christ and the world at large, God has relied on the elemental components to reveal the spiritual times and seasons. The elements have been speaking and prophesying of the emergence of a new generation; they have been prophesying of a Kingdom revolution that is yet to overtake this earth. The elements have been resounding the alarm that the end of this age is nearing, and the coming of our Savior, Jesus Christ, is at hand.

Anytime humanity enters a new age or era, if the prophets do not speak of it, then the elements will. The elements send us signs of what's happening in the spirit realm. If there's unrest in this natural world, so it is in the spiritual. The traffic system compares with this as well. Because drivers aren't capable and responsible enough to react with self-regulating commands to other traffic, there has to be a system of signs and traffic lights in place. These tell drivers what to do on the road. It has also been this way in the realm of the spirit. Because many people have not fully taken their place as sons and daughters of God and have not taken their rightful place of authority, God Himself has instructed the elements to give us signs.

Romans 8:19 (AMPC) says, "For [even the whole] creation (all nature) waits expectantly and longs earnestly for God's sons to be made known [waits for the revealing, the disclosing of their sonship]." In other words, all nature is sending a message to God's sons and daughters. It was never God's original intent for nature to dictate to humans; it was always His plan for us to dictate or speak to nature. Romans 8:22 (AMPC) declares, "We know that the whole creation [of irrational creatures] has been moaning together in the pains of labor until now." When the prophets arise and take their authority, the elements will obey and the earth's pains of labor, its response to making way for the sons and daughters of God, will cease!

Shaking in the Earth

The earth is the largest of the terrestrial planets in our solar system. (The planets Mercury, Venus, Earth, and Mars are called terrestrial because they have compact, rocky surfaces.) Earth is home to literally millions of species, which include humans. The earth is said to be one of the four elements in ancient and medieval philosophy and in astrology.[5] The dictionary also insists that earth is the substance of the human body.[6] This would mean that we are earth! Through the ages, the earth has been called Planet Earth, the world, and terra. *Terra* comes from the Latin word that means land or territory.[7]

Let's take a look at what Scripture says about humankind and the earth. Genesis 1:26 (KJV) says, "And God said, Let us make man in our image, after our likeness: and let them have dominion over the fish of the sea, and over the fowl of the air, and over the cattle, and over all the earth, and over every creeping thing that creepeth upon the earth." This reaffirms humanity's

God-given dominion upon the earth. *Dominion* in the Hebrew is *radah*, which means to dominate, tread down, rule, and subjugate.[8] These meanings simply reveal that we were given authority over the entire earth and everything within it.

Because the earth belongs to the Father, He has committed it into the hands of His children. This means that the people of God have been given jurisdiction over the earth. However, anything that God loves and blesses, the devil tries his best to pervert. For many years, it has been the witches and warlocks who have used nature and the elements to perform their rituals. They have viewed the earth as something sacred that could be used in their evil craft. This goes all the way back to the Old Testament. Many people of that time would use the earth and the elements to worship other gods and perform wicked signs and wonders.

Nevertheless, when Jesus came on the scene, He confounded and astonished the religious leaders of His time. He did things that were considered unorthodox, but He was showing people who has the dominion. In the book of John, Jesus encountered a man who couldn't see because he had been born blind. What Jesus did confounds religious leaders even to this day:

> When He had said these things, He spat on the ground and made clay with the saliva; and He anointed the eyes of the blind man with the clay. And He said to him, "Go, wash in the pool of Siloam" (which is translated, Sent). So he went and washed, and came back seeing.
>
> John 9:6–7

I believe that Jesus commanded the clay or dirt to heal. This is a true example of the type of anointing and authority that the prophets of God have. Prophets have been given the right and permission to utilize the elements. In fact, as a believer, you don't have to hold the office of a prophet to do this. So what was Jesus doing? He was taking back the rights given to God's people. We have allowed the wicked (witches, warlocks, and psychics) to take the place God's prophets are supposed to have. This is why you don't see many prophets and prophetic people using the earth or elements as Jesus did. The people of God don't realize the scope of their dominance.

Prophets and prophetic people don't realize the resources God has given them.

Galatians 4:1 (KJV) states, "Now I say, That the heir, as long as he is a child, differeth nothing from a servant, though he be lord of all." This Scripture reveals that as long as the people of God are underage and immature, although they are heirs, they are no different from a servant. *Child* in the Greek is *nepios*, which means a minor, childish, untaught, and unskilled.[9] Many in the Body of Christ are unskilled and untaught in this area regarding their ability to command and proclaim to the elements. As this Scripture informs us, although believers have the right, because they are untaught and unskilled, it means nothing. God is bringing the Body of Christ into another paradigm of maturity. It is time for you to realize the dominion you have. When you realize that you are the rightful owner of the earth, then the inheritance God has for you will be yours!

A Sound of Abundance of Rain

The prophet Elijah was most certainly a prophet to the elements. As a prophet of God, he understood the significance of releasing God's word to the elements, and they obeyed him. First Kings 17:1 declares, "And Elijah the Tishbite, of the inhabitants of Gilead, said to Ahab, 'As the LORD God of Israel lives, before whom I stand, there shall not be dew nor rain these years, except at my word.'"

Wow, do you mean to tell me that God trusted His servant Elijah that much? So much that Elijah could stop the rain at his word? This lets me know that Elijah understood his authority as a prophet of God. I don't know if you understand the entire scope of his prophetic decree. This meant a whole region would be in a drought for years. This prophetic decree affected the population, the economy, and the food supply! These are areas the elements greatly affect. These are also areas in which God has assigned His prophetic people.

Water is essential to human life and survival. Without it, there's no possible way for humanity to be sustained. When God allows the heavens to be shut by the mouths of His prophets, He is trying to send a message to the entire affected area. Although Elijah prophesied a devastating drought, the prophet was not affected:

> Then the word of the LORD came to him, saying, "Get away from here and turn eastward, and hide by the Brook Cherith, which flows into the Jordan. And it will be that you shall drink from the brook, and I have commanded the ravens to feed you there."
>
> 1 Kings 17:2–4

If a prophet or prophetic person is in right standing with God, He will not allow that individual to be harmed by atmospheric conditions. You may even be the one to prophesy to the elements, but you will not be affected. As the Word of God demonstrates, Elijah was given water to drink and food to eat, while everyone else suffered.

Finally, Elijah had received the word from God to release rain: "And it came to pass after many days that the word of the LORD came to Elijah, in the third year, saying, 'Go, present yourself to Ahab, and I will send rain on the earth'" (1 Kings 18:1). It's important that you wait to hear from God before you release His word. Elijah was under God's authority when he commanded the heavens to be shut. Although Scripture says that by Elijah's word it would not rain, he was still in God's will. When you are connected with God, you'll be able to discern the will of God. You'll know what God permits you to do and what He doesn't permit. A prophet cannot just run around commanding things, as he or she wills. There are spiritual guidelines to follow when you operate under a prophetic anointing. You must be connected to God to know what to do and what not to do.

On this earth there are guidelines and protocols. *Protocol* means the official procedure or system of rules. For example, if you have any sense, then you know that if you place your finger in a socket, you run the risk of being electrocuted. If you stand in the middle of a busy highway, you run the risk of getting hit by a car. It's the same in the spirit realm. There are boundaries to every level of access and authority. As a mature Christian, you must know your prophetic boundaries. The power to command is not something to be taken lightly. It is an awesome responsibility we have been so fortunate to receive.

Furthermore, Elijah went and brought the word to Ahab that it was going to rain (see 1 Kings 18:1–2). I'm sure you probably know the story of how Elijah told his servant to look up in the sky, because it was going to rain. At first the servant didn't see anything. The seventh time he looked, however, the servant saw a cloud the size of a man's hand. At first it was a small cloud, but nevertheless, it was still a cloud. And just as the prophet declared, it most certainly did rain!

I believe that God has placed the element of water into the hands of His prophets. When we speak to the heavens under God's anointing, they must obey. Recently, the area I am from had been under a severe drought. Our water supply was dwindling by the day. We had well under one hundred days of water supply left. The remaining days got down so low that our local government began to panic. During that time, I was in a service where I had to minister. I remember God telling me to declare to the heavens and to the people that the drought had come to an end. I remember wondering and asking God, *Are you sure?*

He reaffirmed His word and spoke to me again. So when I got up to speak the word, I remember stepping into an unusual realm. I don't quite know how to explain it, but there's an unusual anointing that comes upon me when I speak to the elements. I don't always feel this anointing; only at times when I know I must prophesy to the elements. So I began to prophesy to the heavens that "the drought is over, and it must rain." I remember the people in the audience screaming and shouting because they believed the word of God. I could feel the gift of faith there.

We went home, and I thought no more of it. I had declared the word from God, even though there was no rain in our forecast. When we turned on the news, however, something interesting was happening with the weather. The weatherman stated that to everyone's surprise, bursts of unexpected showers were now being picked up on radar. All of a sudden, it started raining in different areas throughout the region. The weather people didn't expect it because it was the supernatural power of God that was causing it to happen. This was exciting! God was letting me know the level of authority that my words have.

The prophetic word didn't just affect my city, but several other surrounding cities and counties. That was very exciting too, but in the next couple of days an analysis was released that said it would take at least three hurricanes coming in order to get us out of this drought. I remember reminding God of His word that the drought was over, and we didn't have to have hurricanes to do it. It was not many days after that when the heavy water restrictions were lifted and the drought came to an end—without the help of any devastating hurricanes!

Storm-Force Winds

Air is so amazing to me! It cannot be seen and you don't know where it comes from, yet it's right there. This reminds me of God. He cannot be seen visibly and you don't know where He comes from or what He will do next, but He's right there! In fact, when you see air in Scripture, it's symbolic of spirit and the Spirit. Acts 2:1–2 says, "When the Day of Pentecost had fully come, they were all with one accord in one place. And suddenly there came a sound from heaven, as of a rushing mighty wind, and it filled the whole house where they were sitting." The Holy Spirit loves to introduce Himself as wind and through wind. In the Greek, the word wind is *anemos*, which means a stream of air, a very strong wind.[10]

Whenever you come into an atmosphere, you can literally release the wind of God to blow. When you do that, you are releasing the Holy Spirit to envelop the atmosphere with His wind. Wind brings refreshing, renewal, and the strength of God. It's the breath of life. It therefore also brings rejuvenation to an individual or group of people.

Now, *wind* in the *Oxford Reference* dictionary means "the perceptible natural movement of the air, especially in the form of a current of air blowing from a particular direction."[11] In Scripture, the Lord is often depicted as moving in a whirlwind. Jeremiah 30:23 declares, "Behold, the whirlwind of the LORD goes forth with fury, a continuing whirlwind; it will fall violently on the head of the wicked." This type of wind represents the violent shaking of God. Many times, it's the judgment of God being released!

There was a season when the Lord had me teaching about the wind. One particular service, the message was entitled "Atmospheric Phenomena." I came from Hosea 8:7 (KJV), which states, "For they have sown the wind, and they shall reap the whirlwind." I began to declare to the people that "whatever you sow into the wind, you shall reap from the wind!" At the end of the message, the Spirit of God began to speak to me concerning tornadoes that would come upon the States. The Lord had me prophesy and release winds of destruction. I declared to the people that in the days to come, there would be tornadoes. The Lord had me release them upon the earth.

I had never done this before, and it was quite shocking to me and, I'm sure, to some of the visitors in the service. However, God said He was releasing His judgment! We recently heard the reports that the year I gave that word was the worst year for tornadoes in its decade. The last report I heard was that over 1,500 tornadoes were sighted, many of them major.

I felt so bad after I had released that word, because I didn't want to scare away people who were visiting our church for the first time. But I've learned that it's better to obey God. When you step out and speak God's word, not everyone will like it. A word of God is not always pretty and charming. Sometimes, it's brutal. Sometimes, God will ask a prophet in our day to speak a hard word, as He did with Old Testament prophets like Jeremiah, Isaiah, Ezekiel, and others.

That's what took place when God had me release the word about tornadoes. A tornado is "a mobile, destructive vortex of violently rotating winds having the appearance of a funnel-shaped cloud and advancing beneath a large storm system."[12] Many times, God will release this type of whirlwind to unearth hidden things in cities, towns, and regions. Contrary to popular belief, God does still release His judgment at times throughout the earth.

Uncontrollable Fire

Fire is a very unique element. It is completely different from the others. Earth, water, and air are all forms of matter. That simply means that they are made up of millions of atoms collected together. However, fire is not matter at all. Fire is the visible, tangible side effect of matter changing form. It is one part of a chemical reaction. Unlike the other elements, in order to have fire there must be some sort of chemical reaction taking place. A typical fire occurs from a chemical reaction between oxygen in the atmosphere and some sort of fuel.

During the time of the prophets of old, God demonstrated Himself often in fire. That's why He is referred to as the consuming fire (see Exodus 24:17; Deuteronomy 4:24; Hebrews 12:29). In 1 Kings 18:22–24, Elijah was coming against the prophets of Baal and challenged them to see whose God (or god) really was God. By the prophet's word, the answer would come by fire:

> Then Elijah said to the people, "I alone am left a prophet of the LORD; but Baal's prophets are four hundred and fifty men. Therefore let them give us two bulls; and let them choose one bull for themselves, cut it in pieces, and lay it on the wood, but put no fire under it; and I will prepare the other bull, and lay it on the wood, but put no fire under it. Then you call on the name of your gods, and I will call on the name of the LORD; and the God who answers by fire, He is God."

Fire would be the sign, and the prophets of Baal started crying out to their god for it: "So they cried aloud . . . And when midday was past, they prophesied until the time of the offering of the evening sacrifice. But there was no voice; no one answered, no one paid attention" (1 Kings 18:28–29). The prophets of Baal had been crying out for hours, and nothing had happened. I believe God wanted to show them who really is the true and living God.

Baal was nowhere to be found when the idolaters needed their god. Would the God of Israel show up for Elijah? Look what the prophet did to make sure everyone would recognize his God (verses 31–35):

> And Elijah took twelve stones, according to the number of the tribes of the sons of Jacob, to whom the word of the LORD had come, saying, "Israel shall be your name." Then with the stones he built an altar in the name of the LORD; and he made a trench around the altar large enough to hold two seahs of seed. And he put the wood in order, cut the bull in pieces, and laid it on the wood, and said, "Fill four waterpots with water, and pour it on the burnt sacrifice and on the wood." Then he said, "Do it a second time," and they did it second time; and he said, "Do it a third time," and they did it a third time. So the water ran all around the altar; and he also filled the trench with water.

Now, by this time Elijah had gone above and beyond what he had previously stated. He added a trench and water to his altar. He wanted the prophets of Baal to see that the God of Israel could bring fire in the midst of water! So Elijah prayed, and the God of fire showed up (verses 37–39):

> "Hear me, O LORD, hear me, that this people may know that You are the LORD God, and that You have turned their hearts back to You again."
> Then the fire of the LORD fell and consumed the burnt sacrifice, and the wood and the stones and the dust, and it licked up the water that was in the trench. Now when all the people saw it, they fell on their faces; and they said, "The LORD, He is God! The LORD, He is God!"

Wow, our God is a consuming fire! In the days ahead, you will see signs of fire being released in the earth. More and more uncontrollable fires will be released as the presence of God consumes that which is not righteous. Not only will this be a sign of God judging the wicked, but it will be a sign that there are fires of revolution and revival being released to certain areas. When the true prophets of God call for the spiritual fire, God will show signs of natural fire upon the earth. This is the word of the Lord for the days ahead!

PROPHETIC INTEL

Storms are going to come, both spiritually and naturally. We will continue to see unusual and disruptive weather phenomena. Some of these will be generated from human science with evil intent, some from the groaning of the earth, and some from God-ordained sources.

How do we tell if the elements are behaving according to a prophetic word or according to a manmade atmospheric system bent on evil? When disruptive weather is of the enemy, it's intention is to push a wicked agenda or to bring destruction. If weather is God-generated, it will have a specific divine purpose behind it. For instance, when I was speaking in a service in Cape Town, South Africa, the area was in a severe drought. God sent rain clouds out of nowhere to replenish the ground. Some would see that kind of abundant rain, flooding, and storms as a disruption, but it was really the hand of God opening the heavens over that region. You will know when a storm is of God because the end result will be to bring life, to judge what is corrupt, or to bring things into God's order.

Whatever the source behind the weather, we can rest assured that Jesus is in the storm with us. Disastrous weather, earthquakes in unusual places, and atmospheric phenomena will get increasingly worse, but I want you to be aware that these are simply signs of the new era and time that we are in. These signs are not the end of the world, but they are pointing to the end of this world as we know it. They reveal to us that our redemption is drawing closer, and that Christ is soon to return. They are also a clarion call for believers to be about our Father's business. We must walk in the purpose He has called us for and win those to the Lord who do not know Him.

9

Food Wars

If you can believe, all things are possible to him who believes.

Mark 9:23

I was traveling in the southeastern part of France. France is actually one of my favorite places to visit. The tourist areas in Paris are great for seeing the historic sites, but when you have a chance to go to the countryside, it's a unique and beautiful experience. When I was there, in a vision I could see a great revival sweeping throughout the region. This would be an outpouring of God's Spirit and the fire of God being released to rekindle passion, unlock harvest, and bring a fresh stirring of the gifts of the Spirit. I quickly focused on the ministerial meetings I was preparing for.

I've been in different parts of France before and have enjoyed the most amazing cuisine. Everything from the melt-in-your-mouth roast duck to the decadent desserts. I'm always enamored with the food creations that come from unassuming, quaint little French restaurants that look like much of nothing, but have, in my opinion, Michelin Star–quality food.

I was in a part of France I had not been to before, so I was eager to get out and see the sites, as well as to enjoy some great food. I decided to go for a hike. As I went walking with a few others, I got caught up in the experience and went several miles beyond what I intended. Now, famished from the hike, the other hikers and I decided to grab a bit to eat. We found the first market we could get to and went inside. They had a grocery section and restaurant deli. I went to the shelves and noticed that they were empty. We searched the whole store, and to my surprise, we found no food. We couldn't seem to get many options from the deli either. I thought to myself, *That's odd. Okay, on to the next.*

I told the people with me, "Let's go down farther; we'll find more options there." We quickly stumbled onto another market. By this time, I was a bit desperate for anything to eat. I hadn't eaten all day and would have taken a bag of chips just to hold me over. We walked into the next store and noticed the same thing—no produce, no meat, no nonperishable items. It seemed mostly empty.

This happened a couple more times before we realized that there must be a shortage. This was eerily similar to a vision the Lord had shown me. I told the people with me that we would see this happen on a much larger scale in nations that you would never have imagined. Why this particular town was seemingly having a shortage, I have no idea. But because I'm a prophet, the Lord will often lead me to places that will emphasize something He has shared with me, or He will even use the experience as a symbol, reminder, or warning of what's to come. I want to share here a few more things He has shown me about the days ahead.

The battles ahead over food and water

In this new era, the new battleground will be over food and water. Food deserts are already widespread, but will become the norm in many communities. A food desert is an area that has limited access to nutritious and affordable food. The Lord showed me that in the days ahead in some once-wealthy countries, there will be times that food will be scarce. I saw gas prices and food prices soaring to ridiculous prices in those times.

In the years to come, the economy and food industry will be completely shaken. This will be a prophetic precursor of Revelation 6:6–8 (ESV):

And I heard what seemed to be a voice in the midst of the four living creatures, saying, "A quart of wheat for a denarius, and three quarts of barley for a denarius, and do not harm the oil and wine!"

When he opened the fourth seal, I heard the voice of the fourth living creature say, "Come!" And I looked, and behold, a pale horse! And its rider's name was Death, and Hades followed him. And they were given authority over a fourth of the earth, to kill with sword and with famine and with pestilence and by wild beasts of the earth.

In addition, in the coming days water, which is so essential to life, will become the most precious and sought-after commodity. In a vision, I saw contaminated water systems. There will be a discovery in many states and regions of disease-causing organisms and toxins in the drinking water. At that time, there will be a public outcry. People will ask, "How did they not know that the water was contaminated?" Because of the mass contamination of some water sources and systems, some nations will battle over water.

Solutionists will arise

The Lord said to me, *Solutionists, strategists, and innovative thinkers will be raised up for that time of crisis.* A solutionist is a problem solver, a person who makes a practice out of figuring out a plan to mitigate difficult situations. This will be the season of problem-solving prophets who will get creative in a time of crisis. They will bring innovation, inventions, and witty ideas that bring relief and hope, and that secure the future of nations. The voice of prophetic creatives must not be silenced in the days that are coming. It's going to take God's intelligence to deal with many of the things that we've never seen before. In the future, prophetic intelligence will be sought after by government leaders and the like to preserve people.

Elisha was a solutionist, a problem-solving prophet. When the city of Jericho cried out because the water was contaminated and bitter, he didn't just prophesy to the people or deliver them a nice speech. With God's prophetic wisdom, he acted. Look what happened: " Now the men of the city said to Elisha, 'Behold, the situation of this city is pleasant, as my lord sees, but the water is bad, and the land is unfruitful'" (2 Kings 2:19 ESV). Some translations say the water was bitter, meaning that it was impure, contaminated, or poisoned. When the city was in trouble, the prophet arose to action:

And he said, "Bring me a new jar, and put salt in it." So they brought it to him. Then he went out to the spring of water and threw salt in it and said, "This is what the LORD says: 'I have purified these waters; there shall not come from there death or unfruitfulness any longer.'" So the waters have been purified to this day, in accordance with the word of Elisha which he spoke.

2 Kings 2:20–22 NASB

This is how we must be in our time. We can't only speak mere words; we must seek God for His knowledge and wisdom to know exactly what to do. I believe God is going to move this way in our time more and more because of the needs that will arise.

These Scriptures give us the key to a powerful combination: Elisha prophesied, and then he did a prophetic act. He put salt in the contaminated water. The salt alone didn't heal the water. It was God's supernatural endowment upon the prophet, along with the salt being a symbol of purification, that healed the water. In our day, there will be things God gives His people to do that won't make sense, but He will be in it. He will use such acts to restore what's broken, heal what's infirm, and free the bound.

You may be reading this and thinking, *It can't be me God wants to use in the coming days.* But I believe you are exactly the person God wants to use to effect change and bring solutions to your community. Remember, nothing is impossible to those who believe (see Mark 9:23).

Vision of artificial foods

In France, I was immediately taken into a vision without warning. I saw store shelves empty and a famine beyond anything I had ever seen in a Western country. I was standing in America in the vision, but didn't even recognize my own country. Stores and restaurants were shuttering, as there was no supply.

Then a white government vehicle, unlike any common vehicle I've ever seen, pulled up on a street where a group of young kids were hanging out. The vehicle had technology affixed to it. I thought to myself, *Maybe it's connecting to a satellite of some sort.*

A lady and a guy got out of the truck and spoke to the children. They said, "We have food for you." It was bread packaged in an odd wrapping. I heard them say to one another that they were experimenting with food that they had created in government labs. The bread was produced with no water and no natural flour. It had a shelf life of five years.

Although this strange bread would temporarily satisfy the hungry children, I knew it would also affect them in a detrimental way in the future. I called out to the children not to eat it. I shouted, *"It's poison!"*

Farming Communities and Storehouses

Whatever the days ahead bring, the Lord has solutions for His people. When the Lord spoke to me to buy a farm, I was flabbergasted. I had no idea where I would get the money or how I would manage it. My realtor, who was not a Christian at the time, showed me the first farm for sale. It was about 45 acres of land. I said to the Lord, *That's too much land. How will I take care of it?*

I stood in the middle of that farm as the Lord stretched my faith to believe Him for it. A few days later, my realtor said, "I've got another farm you need to see. It's more than double the first one."

"Why do you want me to see a farm that's double the size of the first one?" I asked my realtor. "Is it cheaper? Is there some kind of deal on it?"

"Well, no . . ." he said, "it's nearly a million dollars."

I went and looked at the farm anyway. It was amazing and had all the things that I desired. I told the realtor I would buy it. I put in my offer, and to my surprise they accepted it immediately. It would take a number of days for the paperwork and the closing, in order to finalize everything. During this short period, my realtor contacted me again, saying, "You have to see this other farm!"

I was quite annoyed at the directive. "What do you mean, another farm? I already have an offer in on the 100-acre farm, and we're preparing to close!" I answered. I declined, and on top of that, I ignored his insistent requests. He continued calling and texting me about it, until I heard the voice of God concerning it. God told me that He was using the unsaved realtor as a sign that my faith was too low.

After hearing from God, I called the realtor back and said I would go see this other farm. I still thought it was the craziest idea. "Well," I asked him, "is this one cheaper?"

"No," he said, "but it's double the size of the one you have an offer in on now."

That's right—roughly 200 acres of a fully functioning commercial farm. I was dumbfounded at that thought of paying that price and managing something that big. Yet when my feet touched the ground, the Lord said to me, *This is your land!*

Out of faith and obedience, I quickly withdrew the offer on the other property and placed an offer on the new property. It seemed supernatural because money began coming in from every direction. I purchased that property and own it today. Since that time, I have purchased other property, but that one was a sign to me.

God said to me, *I'm allowing you to purchase this as a Joseph storehouse for the coming days. You will call the name of the land Goshen.*

He went on, *This is a sign of what is to come. Joseph storehouses, farms, and Christian communities with resources will be strategically placed throughout the world for the days of disaster and famine that are coming.*

I didn't know the first thing about farming, let alone have a multimillion-dollar budget to buy the kind of farm that I envisioned. It was a long journey, yet God brought the knowledge and insight that was needed. He will do the same for you if you are called to build communities with food, resources, and materials. In the near future, a spirit of unity will come upon believers for such Kingdom collaboration. Group economics will be the wave of the future as groups of friends, families, and even churches will come together to own farms, shared communities, and storehouses.

The Proper Diet for Your Destiny

There is wickedness at the highest levels of the systems and industries that run our world. Specifically, the food and drug industries. As the world moves into a new period of time, you will hear more and more about recalls and contaminated packaged foods. The enemy's plan is to spread disease through an industry that is so vital to life. For this reason, I believe that the Holy Spirit is focusing many people in the Body of Christ on physical health, as well as soul wellness. According to 3 John 2, God desires that we prosper and be in good health. We have a key role, however, in seeing the manifestation of this word. We must partner with the Holy Spirit to see the fullness of His desire come to pass.

In the days ahead, we're going to have to be very particular and Spirit-led concerning what we consume. We will see harmful lab-grown meats, and overprocessed and artificial foods that may be detrimental to the body. I believe it's in our best interest to steer clear of these types of foods and to gravitate toward fresh produce, organic, pure, not grown in a lab, and not genetically modified. We can derive several important points regarding our eating from Scripture:

- "Do you not know that your bodies are temples of the Holy Spirit, who is in you, whom you have received from God? . . . Therefore honor God with your bodies" (1 Corinthians 6:19–20 NIV). This Scripture reveals that our bodies are made to house the Holy Spirit. We must not defile our bodies with the practice of sin. We are also called to honor God through eating healthy.

- "I give you every seed-bearing plant on the face of the whole earth and every tree that has fruit with seed in it. They will be yours for food" (Genesis 1:29 NIV). This denotes that those foods that are grown from out of the ground (fruits and vegetables) are healthy to our bodies.

- "While they were eating, Jesus took bread, and when he had given thanks, he broke it and gave it to his disciples, saying, 'Take it; this is my body'" (Mark 14:22 NIV). This verse connects the natural with the spiritual. Jesus led the disciples into Communion, showing that what we eat in the natural may hold spiritual significance and impact us on a soul level. He also showed them on many occasions the importance of giving thanks to the heavenly Father and praying over your food.

- "It is better not to eat meat or drink wine or to do anything else that will cause your brother or sister to fall" (Romans 14:21 NIV). Don't allow what you consume to become a hinderance to the faith of your brother or sister in Christ. Eating is often communal and can have an effect on others. This is another verse that connects our eating to our faith. Through the apostle Paul, God is admonishing us to make healthy eating choices and to be considerate of the convictions of others.

- "If you find honey, eat just enough—too much of it, and you will vomit" (Proverbs 25:16 NIV). This verse shows us the principle of moderation. Too much of anything may be bad for you, and your body will attempt to push it out. This Scripture further implies self-control, discipline, and governance over what we consume.

| PROPHETIC INTEL |

There is an evil battle taking place over food and water. This will escalate in the coming days. What many are consuming is harming them due to poisons and genetically modified components, among other toxins. God is giving His people discernment to know what to consume and what to discard. The Lord said to me, *Joshua, I'm giving you a diet for your destiny.*

I thought, *Lord, I don't want to be restricted in what I eat.*

He then began to show me specific things that were harmful to me and how I needed to limit them in my daily consumption. In addition, He led me to begin researching foods from the Bible that have healing components. I researched the Mediterranean diet and the diet God's people ate while in Africa (Egypt) during and after the famine. They were farmers and knew how to work the land and eat naturally from the land. Through this experience, God had me limit processed foods and eat from the land. This is a work in progress for me, and I noticed a significant difference after I began implementing what God had shown me.

I encourage you to seek God about the proper diet for your destiny. What you consume matters. God cares so much about you that He wants you to have the best. Here are a few concrete steps you can take to move in that direction:

1. Take a few minutes to evaluate what percentage of your diet currently consists of prepackaged or artificial foods. What two or

three things can you do to reduce that percentage and increase the percentage of freshly grown foods you consume that are healthier for you?

2. Do you grow any of your own foods? Even apartment dwellers with small patios can grow a lot of produce in a container garden. What can you do to learn to be more self-sufficient in the area of fresh food production?

3. Revisit the important points regarding our eating that we drew from Scripture. Which verses stood out to you as ones that you need to apply more consistently in following the diet of destiny God has for you?

10

Economic Collapse

Your heavenly Father knows that you need all these things. But seek first the kingdom of God and His righteousness, and all these things shall be added to you.

Matthew 6:32–33

I can still hear the honking of horns, the sounds of endless chatter, the humming of engines of all sizes, and the piercing shrill of cars slamming on their breaks. All of this was at 2:00 a.m.; that screeching sound is still cemented in my brain. I was in the city that never sleeps, Manhattan, New York. That year, I was in New York so many times that I got used to all the noise and grew to love it. On this particular occasion, I was in the financial district. It's a little bit more peaceful on that side, not too far from Central Park. After conducting business during the day, I would take walks or even bike rides in the park, this small patch of green in the middle of the concrete jungle. The whole experience was surprisingly exhilarating.

By this point, I had preached in New York many times and knew great ministries there. However, this occasion was different. I knew something significant was on the horizon. I could feel it in my bones. I was there for an economic summit. As a prophet, there are times I am called outside the four walls of the Church, beyond the traditional landscape of religion, and thrust into current events or the world system. I was there to speak prophetically to the state of the economy. Sometimes God will use prophets to forecast (that is, to predict or foretell what is to come), to shift the economy by decreeing His will in the midst of a financial crisis, or to release solutions for ominous times ahead.

The economic summit was informative and merged secular leaders with Christian leaders. Since that experience, I have met financial leaders and high-level businessmen and women from around the world. I have had the privilege of doing consulting with some and ministering the word of the Lord. While in New York, I had two jolting encounters that shook me to my core. I went to the Federal Reserve Bank of New York, and to the New York Stock Exchange. At the time, God spoke to me and said, *You must go to these significant places so that I can show you in detail what is to come.*

As I stood in front of the New York Stock Exchange, the Lord spoke again. I can still hear His words now: *America will go through an unprecedented economic shaking, beyond what the nation has seen in its history. When it happens, you will know it. It will not just be a recession or a depression. It will be an economic crash and collapse of the economy that will shift the nation forever. This will be a long and drawn-out period of agony for the United States. Out of the financial ruins will emerge a new thing [says the Lord]. I will break the idolatry and the worship of money. I will cause the nation to humble herself and come back to Me. I will use the crisis for good. After this unprecedented economic shaking, the nation as you have known it will be no more. Yes, America will still stand, but it will not be the same; a new thing will come forth in the United States. This period will be met with outpourings of My Spirit. My people will receive solutions and supernatural provision during this time.*

I was startled by what I heard and saw. The Lord showed me the worst financial crisis in American history coming. This will be devastating to many as the stock market crashes. Many large companies will shutter, some businesses will fold, and the government will be in crisis management mode. When you see these things, it's not over. God still has a bright future for His people, and we will not be destroyed because systems fail. I want to share a few visions with you about the financial changes and challenges ahead.

Vision of a banking shake-up and DeFi surge

As I stood in front of the Federal Reserve Bank of New York, in a vision I saw a time coming where the banking industry will be shaken. Some of your largest banks will fail and shutter. There will be talks once again of government bailouts, but this time it won't go as expected. The Lord allowed me to go to the Federal Reserve bank as a sign. It represents this nation's financial institution. There are twelve Federal Reserve banks of the United States. The Federal Reserve Bank of New York has fourteen above-ground levels and five levels underground. The gold vault in this building contains the largest monetary gold reserve known in the world. I would come to know that God sent me there as a prophetic sign that the economic systems of the world are about to shift. What happens in America will cause a ripple effect throughout the nations. Many nations will experience economic havoc, and people will look to God for answers.

In the near future, we will see the surge of decentralized finance, or DeFi. Many believers who get involved with and invest in DeFi components will see a great return on their investment.

What is DeFi? It's an emerging digital ecosystem allowing people to make purchases, as well as send, exchange, and receive financial assets, all without relying on banks, traditional exchanges, or brokerages. It includes cryptocurrencies, blockchain technology, and other software that allows people to transact business with each other financially.

This is the framework for the new monetary system that will emerge. Digital currency will begin to take over the world. It will be the wave of the future. People will no longer think of money as just paper bills and coins. Money will be seen as digital assets and tokens.

Vision of the rise of a one-world currency

After the decline of the dollar, the financial institutions as we know them in America and other nations will be in transition. The birth of an entirely new monetary system will be upon us. Before these things fully occur, you will see the BRICS nations (Brazil, Russia, India, China, and South Africa) pick up steam and build great momentum. Many other nations will begin to join their endeavors to end the era of the dollar.

Unfortunately, in the vision from God, I saw these nations succeed in that agenda. Not because they are so powerful, and not because they have outwitted the United States and Western nations. They will succeed because God has allowed it in order to fulfill Bible prophecy and to usher the world into a new era. Yes, it will be a sign of judgment to the West, but the implications of this are far greater. The dollar will no longer be the reserve currency of the world. Much conflict, war, and fighting will ensue (see chapter 13 on World War III for more details).

I was conducting a meeting on the future of digital currency with experts and leaders in the finance industry. These were Christian leaders who had come together to advise believers on how to navigate the rapid changes coming to the economy. In that meeting, the Lord spoke to me of the coming one-world currency. He said, *Many Bible prophecy teachers have discerned and interpreted it wrong. The one-world currency will be a group of currencies. Digital and cryptocurrencies are the framework for this global exchange.*

When I heard this, my eyes were opened. God further said to me, *The one-world currency will not be as many have thought; it is already here in seed form. It is a group of digital currencies that will have many faces and will be called by several names. These digital currencies will be used globally and will unite all nations under a false banner of peace.*

This currency won't be backed by the banks of one nation, or by a centralized government. The value of the currency won't be predicated upon the GDP (gross domestic product) of a certain nation. This one-world currency will be untethered from the traditional backing of a single nation, unlike the currency we have known before. There will be wicked people in high places controlling and manipulating the direction, flow, and operation of this global network and exchange.

Although decentralized finance or DeFi will rise, you will see a new reformation and restructuring of the world bank. It will be more visible in the years to come. As other banking systems fail, this one will climb.

A new credit system revealed

The Holy Spirit revealed to me that the coming economic deconstruction will bring a shift to our normal way of buying. I saw the credit system in America change. It will also begin to be adopted more and more in other nations.

This new system of scoring will not be predicated solely on your ability to pay your bills on time or properly manage your debt-to-income ratio. Due to an increased obsession with surveillance and control, governments will begin to monitor your social media and online presence. If you are seen as engaging in what society deems as hate speech, it will affect your economic status.

In addition, portions of the Bible will be deemed as hate speech by a vast majority of society, and even by those within government. This will be a dangerous time in history as the antichrist spirit rages throughout the nations. This will not start out full-blown. Over time, it will change and develop after a great period of economic crisis.

People will be scored by their class and social status. Their scores will be impacted by the secular agendas that they embrace, as well as by the companies, schools, and other organizations that they ascribe to or even work for.

Supernatural Provision

Despite the chaos in the financial markets, the hand of the Lord will be moving with great provision for His people. While some businesses are tanking and some sit in financial ruin, Kingdom entrepreneurs will arise. Many new millionaires and multimillionaires will be birthed. Some will see mega increase from key investments, while others will see ideas, products, and business endeavors from God.

Many believers will experience the best of times in the worst of times. Those within the Church will be anointed like Joseph to become store-houses and hubs for others. Miracles of multiplication will become com-monplace. People will see finances come supernaturally. Some will see food multiply right before their eyes.

You can be confident in knowing this: *God will take care of His people.* He always has, and He always will. This is our promise in Matthew 6:25–33:

> Therefore I say to you, do not worry about your life, what you will eat or what you will drink; nor about your body, what you will put on. Is not life more than food and the body more than clothing? Look at the birds of the air, for they neither sow nor reap nor gather into barns; yet your heavenly Father feeds them. Are you not of more value than they? Which of you by worrying can add one cubit to his stature?
>
> . . . For after all these things the Gentiles seek. For your heavenly Father knows that you need all these things. But seek first the kingdom of God and His righteousness, and all these things shall be added to you.

| PROPHETIC INTEL |

After the decline of the dollar and the rise of digital currency and a one-world network or system, you must realize that God is still going to take care of you. Your faith should not be tied to a currency. Yes, we want our currency to prosper and continue to thrive. But in the case where it does not, we will still have the supernatural provision of God. We live under heaven's economy!

Because you understand this, the Lord will show you how to pivot. Elijah prophesied a drought, and the economy in the region tanked as the drought afflicted the land. Elijah listened to God's instructions and made a pivot. He went to the brook or stream, and the Lord sent ravens to feed him (see 1 Kings 17:1–6). Some theologians believe that "ravens" were a name given to food smugglers who came to supply him every day.

Ravens are dirty birds known as scavengers. Whether Elijah's suppliers were human smugglers or the actual birds, the Lord used something dirty, unconventional, and unclean to help Elijah.

As it was then, it will be the same way now. God will use people who are "unclean" and outside the Church to bring provision for believers and to collaborate with the Kingdom of God. He will use the most unlikely people to bring resources, finances, and provision for you. Prepare yourself to be blessed by those in secular society.

AI and the Beast System

Then I stood on the sand of the sea. And I saw a beast rising up out
of the sea . . .

Revelation 13:1

The sun was scorching hot that day, and I could feel a warm breeze blow
past my face. Although it was normally dry in this part of the world when
inland and not near the coast, this time it felt a little more dry than normal. The whole region was in the middle of a heat wave. I was standing in
Athens, Greece. It was the ancient city where Paul had preached his famous
message in Acts 17, addressing the unknown god whom the people there
worshiped. He addressed how the people of that day worshiped their bodies, the creation, and other things above the Creator.

Standing there, I could still see the ancient ruins and the very monuments
that Paul had seen with his own eyes. I'm a Bible nerd, so being in these
places, seeing these biblical sites, invigorates me. I was scheduled to do
ministry in Athens in a few days, but first I would pass through the islands
of Santorini and Mykonos. The Greek islands are some of the most beautiful you can imagine. You're surrounded by the deep blue sky, and emerald
and turquoise waters. There are tiny white buildings scattered about, set
off by their colorful rich-blue doors, lattices, and roofs.

I flew directly to Mykonos so I could spend as much time as possible there. Everybody who lives or vacations in Greece knows that lost luggage is a common problem when flying to the islands. I didn't get the memo, however, and you guessed it—my luggage didn't make it. I stayed several days on the island with no luggage. I shopped every day for clothing, toiletries, and necessities. Although at first it was frustrating, somehow it became freeing. I sensed that God would use the inconvenience to order my steps to where I needed to be.

After an amazing stay, it was time to head to the next Greek destination. I couldn't imagine getting on a plane and losing my luggage again. I decided to take a ferry ship around the islands from then on. My group and I rushed to the port and found hundreds of people waiting on the dock to board. When the ship came alongside, huge doors opened forward and slammed to the ground. You could hear the sound of screeching metal. Hundreds of people began running onto the ferry. Cars and trucks were also lined up and began driving onto the ship. I had never seen anything like it. My group and I ran frantically, rolling suitcases and cramming through the crowd to make it onto the ship. It was stressful and exhilarating all at the same time.

Sailing the Aegean Sea was something out of this world. My luggage being lost had completely changed my route. I was now headed toward a group of islands. Just before me in the distance was the island of Patmos. As a prophet, there are certain places I travel to that transport me into another realm. This was one of them. I began to pray and felt as though I was immediately taken into another world. The Lord began to show me glimpses of the future, while immersing me in the rich history of the past.

It's believed that the apostle John and Mary, the mother of Jesus, made it to Ephesus. It was there that John became the leader of the Ephesian church. He was captured by the Roman emperor Domitian in a persecution campaign and was eventually sentenced to the island of Patmos.[1] In Revelation 1:9–11 (ESV), John wrote,

> I, John, your brother and partner in the tribulation and the kingdom and the patient endurance that are in Jesus, was on the island called Patmos on account of the word of God and the testimony of Jesus. I was in the Spirit

on the Lord's day, and I heard behind me a loud voice like a trumpet saying, "Write what you see in a book and send it to the seven churches, to Ephesus and to Smyrna and to Pergamum and to Thyatira and to Sardis and to Philadelphia and to Laodicea."

Ancient Patmos was a place where many of Rome's criminals were sent to serve prison sentences in labor camps. John would have been in some of the worst, most harsh conditions anywhere. Patmos was rocky, small, and strikingly barren. Yet it was there that John had supernatural encounters with Jesus Christ. He was caught up in the Spirit and was shown thousands of years into the future.

The Seven-Headed Beast

Throughout the entire book of Revelation, John mentions *the beast*. Further, he speaks of four distinct beasts. Two of the beasts he mentions in Revelation 13 unveil biblical prophecy and the unfolding of world events.

John describes a precise and vivid vision of a beast that comes up out of the sea. It appears that John was standing on the sand of the sea, peering out into the deep. This is either an open-eyed vision, or he was taken up into the realm of the spirit. We don't know whether John was in his body or was having an out-of-body experience, but he describes a beast that has seven heads and ten horns (see Revelation 13:1–2). It was in the form or appearance of a leopard, but its feet were like a bear's, and its mouth like a lion's. On the horns were ten crowns, and on each head were blasphemous names. He is describing one of the most monstrous, hideous, and vile creatures.

John's vision connects to the vision of four beasts that the prophet Daniel had (see Daniel 7:1–8). There, the prophet describes one beast like a lion, one like a bear, another like a leopard, and then the last beast as a combination of all of them. In Daniel's vision, these beasts may have been a symbol of four monarchies.

Both John and Daniel mentioned leopards, which are hunters and scavengers known for their swiftness and climbing ability. Leopards designate their territory by leaving marks and scratches on trees, as well as by leaving urine scent to warn others to stay away. They are known to stick to their strictly demarcated territories. They rarely trespass into other territory. They seem to understand nature's protocols. By looking at the leopard's characteristics, we gain potential insight into how this beast described in Revelation 13 may operate in the world. Further, leopards have dark spots that experts use to identify different individuals, similar to a human fingerprint. Each leopard shows up with distinct fur markings unique to only that particular leopard. They also dwell in the tops of trees and branches. Prophetically, this represents high places. Territorially, the beast in Revelation ascends to high places and systems of the world, and even into government, bringing its wickedness with it.

It's important here to see this beast of Revelation as a system and not just a force. A system is an intricate network of components working together. The heads of this beast having ten horns with ten crowns, and having blasphemies on his heads, speaks to its corruption, evil, and enmity against the true and living God. Likewise, the coming beast system, which is already in the world, will set itself against all things righteous, holy, and godly. It will seek to withstand morality and God's law.

Another thing about leopards is that they can see seven times better than humans. They are nocturnal animals, most active at night. During the day, they are camouflaged in the trees and are hidden in plain sight. In the same manner, this beast system is hidden in plain sight. Most of the world is blind to it. This system becomes even more active during great darkness and night seasons in the world.

Both John and Daniel also mention bears. Let's look at some bear traits to see how they play into this intricate network. Bears are known for their brute strength and massive force. They are defensive animals that protect what they believe is theirs at all costs, even to the point of bringing destruction and killing. In verse 2 of Revelation 13, John references the feet of the beast: "Now the beast which I saw was like a leopard, his feet were like the feet of a bear . . ." Why would this beast have the feet of a bear? Bears have massive claws on their feet that they use for gripping prey. Their feet are wide, flat, and long to help them with traction when they run or climb trees, or even move on ice. It's interesting to note that bears are one of the few animals that walk flat-footed like humans do, rather than walking on their toes. This allows them to stand up on two legs and walk upright, just like people. This is a prophetic indicator of this beast system being able to be versatile in two realms. It is able to shape-shift into the affairs of people, including world systems, governments, and nations, and then shift back into its spiritual beast mode.

Revelation 13:2 further states that the beast's mouth is "like the mouth of a lion." A lion's mouth is extremely symbolic of the type of destruction this system will cause. A lion typically has thirty teeth designed to cut through tough, rough, and calloused skin and tendons. Those teeth rip, tear, and break apart the lion's prey. A lion's teeth are so strong that they aren't even really suitable for chewing, so lions tend to swallow their food in large chunks. The lion's mouth is a sign of the beast being a weapon against humanity, bringing anguish and calamity for a period of time in the earth.

This Frankenstein of a beast will be given authority from Satan, referred to as the dragon in Revelation 13. Satan gives this beast and its beastly system three things:

1. *Power*—The beast will have brute force, influence, and dominance in the world systems. Every worldly industry and structure will be contaminated by its evil. It will be intermingled with society and disguised in enticing, seducing, and electrifying appeal. Its power, however, will come from the devil. Those who bow to it will be influenced by the same wickedness that is oppositional to the plans and purpose of God for humanity. This power will lead to insatiable lust and perversion.

2. *A throne*—The beast will be given a throne, a seat of prominence and notoriety to captivate people. A throne in Scripture is a fixed position from which power flows. The god of this world, the devil, will deceive people into worshiping this beast, this enemy and its system. People wouldn't readily worship something that looks the way that the book of Revelation describes this unusual being. However, it will be disguised. The Bible uses the beast as an allegory to show the spirit of the age that will be at work in the world. This beast is a culture, a perverted belief system, and an invisible force.

3. *Great authority*—In Scripture, the beast is given the permission, ability, and right to govern in the world. The Bible uses the phrase *great authority*, denoting that this demonic force will be exalted by the world system and will greatly influence those who follow it. As John wrote,

> Then I stood on the sand of the sea. And I saw a beast rising up out of the sea, having seven heads and ten horns, and on his horns ten crowns, and on his heads a blasphemous name. Now the beast which I saw was like a leopard, his feet were like the feet of a bear, and his mouth like the mouth of a lion. The dragon gave him his power, his throne, and great authority. And I saw one of his heads as if it had been mortally wounded, and his deadly wound was healed. And all the world marveled and followed the beast. So they worshiped the dragon who gave authority to the beast; and they worshiped the beast, saying, "Who is like the beast? Who is able to make war with him?"
>
> Revelation 13:1–4

The Beast System Is Here

The beast is part of the culmination of things in this world. But before it fully manifests, this beast system and framework will already be at work in the earth. In fact, it's here now. More now than ever, this invisible demonic system is all around us. It is a system that empowers religion, tradition, and worldly ambition—devoid of God and His holiness. It is a system that promotes secular humanism and the idolizing of self. It will endorse and foster satanic agendas and things that are contrary to the will of God.

Further, the beast system is a system of control. It usurps individual authority by slowly taking away freedoms and injecting itself into every part of human life and experience. This will largely be done through the vehicle of artificial intelligence (AI). AI is technology that enables computers, software, digital programs, and machines to simulate human functions or intelligence by carrying out human tasks and problem solving, often at a rate much faster and more efficient than humans.

AI in and of itself is not evil. It will do much good by advancing production in companies, perfecting medical procedures, and even allowing us to travel, work, and do life more effortlessly. That's the desensitizing allure of this initial euphoric phase of AI. It will seemingly make life better. The Church will use it to spread the Gospel of Jesus Christ and effect real change around the world. Good will come out of it as we advance the Kingdom of God.

AI will also be used by the world, however, to advance a satanic agenda. Wicked leaders have already wielded it to control, restrict, and direct the population. Soon AI will become unmanageable and unruly, and will be the driving force of the beast system. *The only way to navigate the tumultuous system and demonic agenda behind artificial intelligence is through prophetic intelligence.*

Prophetic intelligence is the mind of God being superimposed on the hearts and minds of believers, giving us access to God's supernatural wisdom, revelation, and capabilities beyond our human ability. In addition, prophetic intelligence unlocks the future through Spirit-led directives and insight showing us what to do for what is coming. I want to share a couple of visions I've had that provide us with such insight for the times ahead.

Vision of buying and selling in the future

In the coming months and years, you will see AI dominate how we buy and sell. The Lord showed me that we won't need credit cards, debit cards, or paper money in the future. Those things will become obsolete. Gone will be the days of lugging your wallet or purse around with you. Everyone will have digital wallets. You won't even need to use your smartphone to pay. Stores will have such sophisticated recognition technology that they will be able to scan the palm of your hand or your eyes. Digital money will then be deducted from your online account.

This system will come with ease and enjoyable convenience. The underlying problem is that people will be more easily monitored. What you purchase will be logged and recorded digitally. And if people present themselves as oppositional to society, their buying and selling ability will be shut down. These monetary features of the beast system will be viewed as a privilege. In the future, this system will be used as a method of control and punishment. I know this seems farfetched, but already we're not far from this vision that the Lord has shown me.

Advanced communication and augmented reality vision

Even clunky smartphones will become a thing of the past. You—*your human body*—will become the hardware by which technology runs. I was transported into the future and saw this vision where I was with others in a store setting. I was talking on the phone, but there was no phone. I couldn't even see a device. I thought this was extremely odd. It's as if I was seeing myself living in that period of time, but I didn't fully understand how things were operating. Everything was done by this extremely small, unnoticeable, wearable device in the hand.

In this vision, I could see images popping up in midair. Clearly, I was in a store or a mall. The images reminded me of 3D glasses or smart glasses, where you can see things that are not there. The odd thing was, no one had on glasses, but we could all see different 3D images and videos. These were like holograms, but you could interact with them. You could swipe, wave your hand, or simulate clicking in midair, but there was no screen. People were able to buy products, sign up for online lists, or even communicate with a person representing the store or product. I could tell that these representatives were not real people, but were AI generated.

In this vision, I was not afraid or alarmed by what I saw. As believers, we should not be afraid of the things to come, nor should we run from or disassociate from technology. We are called to be light in the dark. We are called to engage with technology and use it as a tool of light.

| PROPHETIC INTEL |

The beast system will expand in every industry, sector, and community in the world. In some ways, this system will seek to push evil agendas to people, but there are ways in which we as believers can counter those efforts and push back.

Artificial intelligence will bring some good, but will also be used to promote control, surveillance, and integration with the human body. We can counter this demonic agenda by using the platform of AI for great things like effecting positive change and contribution. We will be able to use new technological advances such as the metaverse to spread the Gospel to a people who would never come into the four walls of a church. Again, believers shouldn't run from technology; we need to use it for the Kingdom.

The beast system will affect our money and financial industries. It will affect how we buy and sell, and it will invade the privacy of our sales and purchases. Digital currency will become the norm as we see the phasing out of fiat currency. To counter this demonic agenda affecting finance, we must confront the spirit of mammon. Mammon is the principality and demonic entity that governs this natural world, and we must not serve it (see Matthew 6:24). Sever your tie with the love of money! Don't chase it or have any affection for it. The love of it is a doorway for the beast system to come through and influence your life. See money just as a tool to accomplish your purposes and further the Kingdom.

The beast system will bring greater persecution upon Christians. You will see attacks, violations of our freedoms, and attempts to harm believers physically at times, due to a growing hatred of God's laws and statutes. Keep in mind that "all that will live godly in Christ Jesus shall suffer persecution. But evil men and seducers shall wax worse and worse, deceiving, and being deceived" (2 Timothy 3:12–13 KJV). You counter persecution by standing boldly for Christ and continuing strong in your faith. Don't allow yourself to compromise and back down from your belief in the whole Word of God.

When evil is growing and trials are mounting in your environment, count it all joy. When temptations and attacks come against you, praise God anyway. Your spirit of praise and joy will oppose the evil agendas of the enemy.

12

Blackout

For behold, the darkness shall cover the earth, and deep darkness the people; but the LORD will arise over you, and His glory will be seen upon you. The Gentiles shall come to your light, and kings to the brightness of your rising.

Isaiah 60:2–3

I ran outside my house to see what all the commotion was about. There was an eerie sense that this was going to change everything. All my neighbors were standing outside in shock, frantically trying to figure out what was going on. There seemed to be some sort of attack. The electricity went out. You could hear the sound of faint booms in the distance. Families didn't know if it was just their individual homes that had lost power, or if a transformer had blown. Only after they went outside did they see that the outage was widespread. This was clearly more than a single neighborhood issue, but just how widespread was it?

In the distance, I could hear and then see the aftereffects of some type of explosion. Law enforcement and special forces were on the streets throughout the city. My mind wondered, *Is this a surprise attack from another country? Are we being invaded?*

It was clear that all power and communication were out. No phones worked. No TVs worked. Smartphones and even the internet were down. This was the beginning of a nightmare situation.

Vividly, I could see a plane that had come down in a suburban neighborhood. The fuselage was on fire. Alarmed, I hoped and prayed that the passengers were able to get off safely! I was horrified at what was playing out right before my eyes. It looked like something out of a movie gone horribly wrong. Although the things that were unfolding were grossly concerning, I could sense the presence and voice of God. He was leading me on where to go and told me exactly what to do.

I ran toward law enforcement to see if I could get any information. They were focused on keeping the crowds of people calm, and they were in search of some sort of threat yet to be discovered. Police dogs were moving around. The scene was bizarre. Just as I turned to go find my family, I noticed that the animals began acting strangely. The pets in the neighborhood, as well as wild birds flying overhead and other wildlife, all started to go berserk. It's as if they could see something invisible that we could not. They were moving around erratically. In that moment, I heard the Spirit of God say loudly, *It's chemical warfare.*

There was an airborne chemical substance that was affecting people, but only the animals could sense it. Immediately, I began to yell out to the people and the authorities, *"It's chemical—the threat is chemical!"*

Quickly, I was carried over to another vivid scene taking place in someone's home. A crowd of people were gathered in the living room. Many were people I knew, along with their families. We were evacuating the area. We were in a blackout. We couldn't use cell phones, the internet, or even electronics. Some types of vehicles powered by elaborate tech would not work. Yet it was as if the Holy Spirit had prepared us. We had supply bags, two-way radios, safety kits, nonperishable items, and supplies for dealing with environmental challenges.

We also had a plan. We were headed to a specific destination. We loaded up and started moving toward the main highway. As we were leaving, we looked back and saw that many people were realizing that they needed to get to a safer place. It was my understanding that this was the scene playing out everywhere. Our group made it out before the gridlock. Cars soon began to jam the highways. I had never seen anything like it. Traffic was beyond halted. Cars and trucks were making additional lanes on the highways, frantically trying to get out. It was chaos. Because of the overload, many cars were stranded. The drivers had either run out of gas or just thought it would be better if they walked.

To me, it looked as if the National Guard had been called up in every state. To my surprise, they had set up a makeshift checkpoint on the main highway and were stopping people from leaving our state. We made it out just in time. The nation was experiencing various attacks. We knew we were in a blackout, and it wasn't going away quickly.

Prophecy of a coming blackout

This is the recurring night vision that the Lord has shown me on several occasions over the past several years. This is a prophetic warning to watch, pray, and prepare.

For some years now, the Lord has given me this prophetic warning of America and other nations becoming the target of a massive blackout. I saw it start to come in the form of small cyberattacks here and there—one company being hit with cyberwarfare, one county being hit in its local government. There is an evil plan, however, to inflict widespread chaos on the masses and cripple governments and entire nations. Intercessors must stand in agreement to pray against the attack, in order to lessen the blow of the enemy, and then pray for the wisdom and insight to know what to do in the midst of the attack.

There will be demonic plots of cyberterrorists and antagonistic regimes to target America's satellites, as well as those of other nations. According to Statista, 5,465 active satellites are orbiting the earth in outer space. Of those satellites, 3,433 belong to the United States.[1] These satellites provide navigation and timing data for the military and citizens alike. They help power our grids, and they keep our society functioning in the way that we know it. These vital satellites are key components of our world. For this reason, they must be secure, guarded, and covered in prayer for a hedge of protection to surround them.

135

Power grids and water supply vision

As I mentioned, in the night vision God showed me cyberterrorists going after our power grids. In that vision, I knew that these diabolical entities had already gained access into our grids, and even into the digital components operating our pipelines and water supply.

I saw a day coming when disruptions to our electrical grids, water supply, and basic necessities of life will become the norm for that period of time. These blackouts will begin to pop up all over. Cities around my nation will experience these disruptions, sometimes seemingly randomly.

I saw where blocks, neighborhoods, and towns will come under cyber-attack. Hospitals, office buildings, banks, municipal buildings, and more will be prime targets.

This may seem hard to believe if you live in a Western nation that has been enjoying comfort, convenience, modern amenities, and the easy flow of operational systems. Yet this period of blackouts will usher us into a time where many of our systems won't function in the way we have grown accustomed to.

Computer glitches and hacks prophecy

Technology is about to advance beyond what we could have ever imagined. It will be exciting and exhilarating. If you are a tech person like me, then using new devices or programs to complete projects, do business, or connect with family is a welcome experience. Simple tasks can be done even faster.

However, more and more computers and tech systems will become the center of major theft and hacks. Due to advanced and skilled hackers, we will see entire organizations compromised. The Lord showed me a period of time in the blackout vision where the internet and phone communications won't work. In that vision, I saw this cause much panic as people were unable to connect with family members or friends. They didn't know what was going on. This wasn't just for an hour or two, but for an extended period of time. This prophecy is one that I give with caution, as a warning of what those with evil plans will seek to put in motion.

I saw computer systems going haywire. People will look in their bank accounts and realize that considerably large amounts of money have disappeared without a trace. Banks will not be able to fully explain what has occurred. Even some of your major apps used for sending and receiving money will be greatly compromised. In this future vision, I saw this happening to large groups of people, and there was no remedy. This will be a time when people will have to be wise with where they put their money. More than anything, people will have to have faith in God and not in manmade systems.

Guard the Gates

This will be a time to watch, pray, and guard the spiritual gates of your city, region, and nation—even the gateway of your mind. God is strategically placing you in your community as a light in the darkness. No matter the chaos or attacks that will be sent against your community, God has placed you there. I speak throughout this chapter about periods of blackouts as they relate to technology and grids, but the real power of God resides on the inside of *you*.

You don't have to worry when you hear all these things. I'm not sharing these prophetic words for you to be in fear. It's the exact opposite—so that you might be warned ahead of time, and so that you might realize your calling in difficult times. You are the light of this world, and you have an important assignment as a believer to guard the gates. If you pray . . . if you intercede . . . if you speak life . . . God will turn any situation around.

That means prayer warriors can cause attacks to bow at the name of Jesus! What the enemy meant for evil, God will turn around for our good. The enemy wants to use these future situations to shake the faith of God's people, and to cause people to panic and experience mental and physical anguish. Instead of that happening, these situations are going to cause the faith of believers to come alive even more. The blackouts will be an opportunity for evangelism and for pointing people to Christ.

God is calling for His people to stand in the gates and war. A gateway is an opening used to transition from one place to another. Spiritually, gates represent entrances to higher levels and dimensions in God. Therefore, the Holy One of Israel is sending His people to war in the midst of transition. Transition is the process of changing from one state or condition to another.

The enemy always fights your transitions because he desires for you to be stuck in the same place. For this reason, you must war or engage the enemy in battle. If you don't fight, then you won't pass through. Matthew 11:12 states, "And from the days of John the Baptist until now the kingdom of heaven suffers violence, and the violent take it by force." This means that God has given His people the power to take authority over the power of the enemy!

The enemy has been regrouping and plotting to figure out a way to keep you from entering into the place God has designed for you. Scriptures reveal that the enemy walks to and fro, seeking to destroy and devour (see 1 Peter 5:8–9). It's his mission to stop you. This is the purpose of the fight going on in the realm of the spirit right now. But when you resist the enemy, standing firm in your faith, you can prevail.

A Clarion Call to War in the Spirit

The winds of war are blowing, and war is stirring in the fortified gates. In other words, you are in your transition period and that's why the war has intensified against you. It is now time for you to stand in the midst of the gates and fight. In the spiritual realm, the horn is being blown for the warriors to storm the gates and fight. It is a clarion call for God's people to arise.

Judges 5:8 (KJV) says "They chose new gods; then was war in the gates: was there a shield or spear seen among forty thousand in Israel?" In this passage, the people had chosen other gods. They put something before God, and this is what brought about the war. Sometimes we cause attacks to come against us because of our own actions. Nevertheless, whatever the reason may be, you have found yourself in the midst of a battle. This could be a financial, emotional, familial, or even a mental battle. Whatever you are facing, you're in a place where you have the choice to give in or to fight your way through. The interesting part about this passage of Scripture is that there is no shield or spear seen among the warriors.

This shows that the battle came suddenly and they didn't have time to prepare. Likewise, the battle you are going through may even have caught you off guard.

Although you also may have been surprised by the attacks of the enemy, all you need to do is depend on God. Judges 5:11 (KJV) declares,

> They that are delivered from the noise of archers in the places of drawing water, there shall they rehearse the righteous acts of the LORD, even the righteous acts toward the inhabitants of his villages in Israel: then shall the people of the LORD go down to the gates.

This Scripture reveals that regardless of the lack of weapons the warriors had, all they did was show up for battle and God fought through them. God will always deliver those who change their wrong ways and allow God to fight through them.

It's very important that you notice the phrase "the noise of archers" in this passage. With this battle, much noise is being sounded. In the Hebrew, *noise* is the word *kole*, and it means a voice or sound.[2] *Archers* in the Hebrew is *khaw-tsats'* and means "to chop into, to pierce or sever; hence, to curtail, to distribute."[3] The enemy is sending a noise to chop and sever. He is sending a piercing noise to split and divide. This noise represents a sound of destruction, terror, and fear. In your personal life, you may be hearing such a noise. Oftentimes, people around you release fear, terror, and destruction just by what they say. You must not allow that noise to affect you! Although the devil may be sending his noise, God *will* deliver! In the place of your greatest struggle, God will always show forth His righteous acts so that you will turn to Him like never before and do His will.

In this Scripture, the writer has also carefully interjected the phrase "the places of drawing water." In the Bible, water is often a symbolism for the Holy Spirit. God will therefore deliver us in the place where His Spirit is. So it's imperative to be in a place that is water accessible (spiritually speaking, as well as in the natural). If there's no water, then there's no deliverance. If you are in a dry place or season, allow the Lord to refresh you with water. Water is vital in order to live. Water brings life and purity in both the natural and spiritual realms. It's impossible to go on without drawing from the water of God.

Judges 5:13 (KJV) proclaims, "Then he made him that remaineth have dominion over the nobles among the people: the LORD made me have dominion over the mighty." This lets us know that those who remain in this fight and stay in place—even though it looks as though not a spear or a shield is in hand—will have dominion. The Hebrew word for *dominion* here is *rawdaw*, which means to tread down, to crumble off, prevail against, reign, bear, make to rule, and take.[4]

Hear me by the Spirit: Those who tread down the enemy, prevail, and bear the weight of this war will have dominion. To tread down means to walk over; it's the concept of having victory over something. If you hold up through this and tread down every stronghold, you will reign in power over the enemy. How? Not by your strength, but by the power of God you will be given authority over mighty strongholds. You fight by using the Word of God as your weapon. That's why there's no need for a shield or spear. We have something far greater than any natural weapon—and that's the power of God!

| PROPHETIC INTEL |

Yes, there will be difficult days ahead in the world. Some of the comforts and conveniences that we've grown accustomed to will be disrupted. Again, I didn't share any of this information to scare you, but rather to warn you so that you can prepare. I believe that we must be prepared spiritually for these challenges by praying, fasting, and reading the Word of God. This threefold cord will build your faith, equip you with spiritual weapons, and keep you grounded in God.

Not only should we do the spiritual preparation, but there are natural things we can do as well. Because God has given us prophetic intelligence, He has anointed our minds to think. He gives us practical things to do that will protect us. Proverbs 2:10–11 (ERV) says "You will gain wisdom, and knowledge will bring you joy. Planning ahead will protect you, and understanding will guard you." Practical wisdom is a defense for God's people, and we should never forget it. God's supernatural power is the combination of the spiritual (super) and the natural.

Prophetically, we are aware that disaster is coming. God has released many prophetic words through His prophets, and more than anything, through His written Word. There are blackouts coming, and we need to know how to prepare. Remember that this is not fear-based information, but preparation. If you knew that a massive hurricane was coming to your city, wouldn't you use wisdom and prepare for it? That's the same way I view these cyberattacks and outages. I'm going to give you a list of items that you may need in case of disaster. This is how the Lord has instructed me to prepare, and I'm passing this knowledge on to you:

- Two-way radios with a long range of several miles (in multiples for you and family members)
- Nonperishable food items
- Gas kept above half full in cars
- RF shielding blanket that keeps electronics safe
- EMP shield
- Dust, medical, and gas masks (to help filter contaminated air)
- Water (one gallon per person per day for several days, for drinking and sanitation)
- Food kept stocked (and at least a several-day supply of nonperishable food on hand, as already stated)
- Battery-powered or hand-crank radio and a National Ocean and Atmospheric Administration (NOAA) weather radio with tone alert
- Flashlight
- First aid kit and a supply ahead of prescription medicine
- Fire extinguisher
- Extra batteries
- Whistle (to signal for help)
- Plastic sheeting and duct tape (to shelter in place)

- Moist towelettes, garbage bags, and plastic ties (for personal sanitation)
- Wrench or pliers (to turn off utilities)
- Manual can opener (for food)
- Local maps
- Cell phone with chargers and a backup battery

13

Clash of Crowns
World War III

> A time to love, and a time to hate; a time of war, and a time of peace.
>
> Ecclesiastes 3:8

I was driven illegally into Syria during a time of great crisis and persecution. We loaded into a Hummer and began riding. I wasn't familiar with any of the terrain. We had been in several Middle Eastern nations, from Lebanon to Jordan and down by the Gaza Strip. The Hummer was so loud you could barely hear yourself think or talk. I was asked several questions on the way. I had to repeat each answer three or four times, shouting louder and louder with each sentence.

This was a stealth mission, I was told. My host in the area, also a great friend for many years, blurted out, "I'm told they are beheading people in this area. They've kidnapped a number of people and are threatening to kill them. We are going there on a prophetic prayer mission, to see them released."

I thought to myself, *This is crazy! I love it!* You see, I was just never the type to be stuck inside the four walls of the Church. I do love ministering and serving in a church; I'm there faithfully most Sundays. But my greater passion and assignment is in the nations. We were going on the kind of mission I thrive in. I'd been in other countries to minister when they were beheading Christians. I remember once when I was headed to a European country, and to my surprise, the pastor there called to tell me that a man had just been gutted with a machete for naming the name of Jesus Christ on the exact train I was supposed to be on. This pastor was frantic as word went out that they were killing Christians.

One time, I was held at gunpoint in a Muslim country because my name is Joshua and they perceived that I was in the Christian faith and doing ministry. Unfortunately, the Lord has shown me visions that this kind of persecution will get worse, and even come to the shores of America and Western nations. We must prepare our hearts and minds for this kind of warfare, and we must believe God for supernatural intervention.

In Syria, the Hummer pulled up to a designated area just across from where the hostages were. My host pointed and said, "That's where they are being kept. Their captors are threatening to kill them within the next 24 hours."

Drones were flying around above us, doing surveillance. Although my friend and host had many weapons, all kinds of guns and ammo, our greatest weapon of protection wasn't some firearm or special earthly defense technology. We had a greater defense technology that can only come from heaven. Our shield was the glory of God. We were told repeatedly that people had just been killed in the very place where we were standing. We did not fear, because we knew that God was with us. We stood there and began to prophesy, as the Lord commanded. We decreed that there would be no beheadings. We canceled the death decree in the realm of the spirit.

I prophesied that the hostages would be released unharmed and untouched. In that moment a visible whirlwind, like a small tornado, formed in front of us. I had never seen anything quite like it in my life. The whirlwind picked up debris and anything in its path. It moved as if it were alive, until it was standing directly in front of us. When we stopped praying and prophesying, it dispersed.

We got word that within 48 hours the hostages were released unharmed, without a single scratch on their heads. The media didn't understand why or how it had happened. We knew that it was the hand of the Lord. The wind of the Spirit had blown through with great deliverance.

An era of war vision

As I journeyed through many areas in the Middle East, the Lord took me into a vision. I saw a great clashing that would come out of Iran, Iraq, Syria, and the surrounding nations. War will rage, and there will be an escalation of things concerning Israel. The spark for World War III will come out of the Middle East.

Whether you know it or not, the world has entered into an era of war. There will be back-to-back conflicts that will erupt in a long and drawn-out war. There is a reordering of nations happening right before our eyes. Nations will choose sides as battle lines are drawn. The Lord has said to me, *My Church is not ready for what is coming; you must prepare them.*

Most of us have never had to live through a major war. We don't understand how taxing it can be on the economy, as well as on the emotional health of an individual. Wartime is never easy, yet it is not the end of the world; it is actually the beginning of a new era. But it will take grit, persistence, and mental fortitude to survive and not succumb to battle fatigue.

Dismantling Three Major Demonic Spirits

In this coming era of war, three major demonic spirits will be released. These three rank higher than an average demonic spirit—more like a principality, or what the Bible calls a throne. They are forces or entities that set up a system, culture, and spiritual governance in the earth. They are invisible to the naked eye and can only be understood through the Holy Spirit.

In order to dismantle these spirits, believers must engage in a strategic plan of prayer and fasting. These three spirits are the spirit of terror, the spirit of destruction, and the foreboding spirit that brings a fear of death. Let's expose each of these spirits and their evil strategies, to gain a better understanding of how to war against them.

The spirit of terror

Terror is a state of intense or overwhelming fear. It is the driving force behind terrorism, which is rooted in fear. The *Oxford English Dictionary* defines terrorism as the unlawful use of violence and intimidation, especially against civilians or a country. It is used to achieve political or ideological goals.[1]

Terrorism is used to gain control or dominance over people on a mental level. Terrorists manipulate others by instigating mental fatigue in them over impending doom or danger. The terrorists will oftentimes announce their plans or state their intentions repeatedly, until people become desensitized. Then when the terrorists actually begin to carry out their agenda, it may go unnoticed until after the action is done. Then they will very vocally claim that they are behind the act.

In this era of war, however, the demonic strategy is *invisible terrorism*. This is a term I've coined to explain a rising threat, where a nation or group of people act violently against others without taking ownership or placing the blame somewhere else. In the world of illusion, it is called sleight of hand or misdirection.

In ancient Chinese culture, this is known as *open feint* in the Thirty-Six Stratagems, a collection of 36 Chinese proverbs that can also be described as military tactics. These proverbs are attributed to Sun Tzu, a Chinese military general and philosopher who lived during the Zhou period. (I should note that many scholars reject the assertation of Tzu being the author, because most of the 36 proverbs are generally regarded as originating after that period.) The *open feint* proverb instructs that to move about in the shadows, in isolation, or even hiding in darkness will make others suspicious. So instead, you must hide in plain sight. You must act out in the open, while hiding your true intentions under the disguise of everyday routine and activities. An enemy masks his true goals by using the ruse of a false intention or a fake goal until his real intention is achieved.

The modern interpretation of this is to act out in the open, but hide your true plans. Tactically, in front of everyone an enemy will point toward the east, when his goal actually lies in the direction of the west. This causes a victim to be caught off guard, and when the attack is successful, the targeted victim becomes shrouded in fear of the next attack. This is how a spirit of terror operates in the earth. It is demonic, diabolical, and unfortunately will cause great intended harm against the West.

The spirit of destruction

The spirit of destruction in our time will act through little wars and sneak attacks. Centuries ago, a successor was on the rise in France by the name of Emperor Napoleon Bonaparte. He gained immediate access to the emperor's position and went about seizing many lands and territories. He was advancing, he was progressing, and he was an impressive, cutting-edge leader. Napoleon's enemy was watching closely, however, observing, planning, and even strategizing. How could this enemy, a lesser power, find a way to immobilize Napoleon and his army, a stronger power? The only way a lesser or smaller power can defeat a stronger, much more advancing power is by *guerrilla warfare*.

Guerrilla in Spanish means *little war*. Through guerrilla warfare, Napoleon's enemy assembled hit-and-run raids and attacked his supply chain. This caused Napoleon's soldiers to become tied up fighting in their own country when Napoleon needed them elsewhere. The supply chain involved a transportation source headed for a specific destination. It moved supplies like food, goods, and equipment to the army, all the necessities needed to sustain life in the midst of a battle. So the enemy found a weakness, a way to break in. Through that weakness, a less powerful enemy was able to immobilize the more powerful entity, Napoleon.

In the spirit, I saw a new wave of terrorism that will move through technology. Through persistent and repeated attacks, cyberterrorists will seek to wreak havoc on our government systems and our convenient way of life. Their target will be our supply chain, production systems, power grids, food supplies, and basic necessities. (We went into some detail about this in the previous chapter.) This is a destructive spirit that seeks to cause injury or harm through broken, perverse, and corrupt people.

The spirit of foreboding and fear of death

This spirit brings a looming feeling of impending doom. It is an evil foreboding, trapping its victims in a constant state of panic, pandemonium, and dread. When the fear of death grips people's minds, they stop living and begin merely existing.

This spirit operates by imbedding itself into a culture by celebrating and exalting things that are of the dead. Even now, the current culture in my country embraces gore, blood, and even killing. In movies and media, there's a seductive fascination with ghosts, demons, devils, and hell. This fascination has crept into clothing and even tattoos, with the incorporation of skulls, dead celebrities, and satanic symbols. What many don't realize is that this is an open door for the fear of death to enter into an entire generation. What looks harmless will have harmful ramifications when the enemy seeks access into people's lives through that open portal.

This era of war will be shrouded with propaganda about impeding danger. This is a type of sorcery that's being planned by the enemy to prepare the land for real despair and danger. The most effective way to combat the fear of death is to understand that if we are in Christ, as believers we are promised life forevermore, beyond this world. Then we must also learn to speak life and decree the life-giving Word of God.

Prophecies of Clashing Crowns

As we close this chapter on clashing crowns and war, I want to share some prophecies about the things ahead. As you read them, remember that "Some trust in chariots and some in horses, but we trust in the name of the LORD our God" (Psalm 20:7 NIV). That word for King David's time is also a word for the time we live in.

An evil shall arise from the East prophecy

The Lord said to me that the nations are gathering in the East against America and Europe. Out of the East will arise technology, weapons, biochemical warfare, and weaponized viruses and diseases that we have never seen. They will target civilians and seek to spread destruction with a new kind of war. This kind of war won't involve artillery lines being drawn. This will be a stealth battle to cripple governmental structures with fear, panic, and a slow infiltration.

I heard God say, *Put your eyes on the Eastern hemisphere.* In the spirit, I saw an east gate open up. This gate was massive and ancient. It looked as if it had been jammed shut for many centuries. All of a sudden, it opened like a lift gate, and a massive army came through it. The Lord said to me, *This is China and the group of nations that she is amassing.* Then I understood—China is in East Asia. An evil is brewing from the diabolic agendas that are being hatched. This is not a word against the beautiful Chinese people. God is speaking specifically about a spirit that will be influencing certain leaders and their ideologies.

The dragon prophecy

I saw a vision of a large dragon. This dragon was humongous, with smoke coming from its nostrils. It was in a raised position and ready to strike. I knew that this represented a nation. This dragon morphed between a flying dragon and a serpent. At times it looked like a dragon, and at other times it looked like a serpent. This dragon began to make war with the eagle, and for a period of time the dragon began to dominate. In this vision I saw the words "*the year of the serpent.*" Then I saw "*the era of the dragon.*"

There will arise a new era of dominance in the world. This will be like nothing we have seen. China and her allies represent the dragon and this system that will rise. We will see the quick advancement and rapid expanse of this cluster of nations. Do not fear and do not be afraid; these things must come to pass for the fulfillment of biblical prophecy.

The forbidden alliance prophecy

The clashing of crowns will continue in the Middle East. There will be periods of silence, but not real peace. The tensions will continue to mount into a massive war. What we have seen with the attacks on Israel and other Middle East nations have just been a precursor of what will reach a boiling point. The hand of the Lord has been holding back the full escalation of war. In a vision from God, I saw this forbidden alliance coming with several nations in the Middle East. It looked as though a peace treaty or deal was being brokered, but the motive of these leaders was deceptive. While they publicly signed in front of the world, their hearts were still deceptive against Israel. The alliance went forward, but it was short-lived. It didn't last.

We have stepped into the age of forbidden alliances. An alliance is a treaty between nations or individuals for mutual advantage. The nations that will come together in the coming years will be shocking to many, but behind the scenes, deals will be made and secret pacts will be forged. Unlikely nations will conspire against America and Israel. Persecution will arise and the world systems will change, but God will move by His power in the midst of it.

PROPHETIC INTEL

The next several years will prove that we have come into an era of war. Wars and rumors of wars will be commonplace. It's imperative that in the midst of war, threats, and attacks, you don't allow yourself to be consumed by a spirit of fear. You must remember that the all-powerful One, the true and living God, is with you. "God has not given us a spirit of fear, but of power and of love and of a sound mind" (2 Timothy 1:7). The spirit of fear comes to attack your power, which is your ability. It attacks your love, which is your commitment and decision to love God and others. Love is the foundation of your faith. It also attacks your mind so that you will make decisions that are not thought out or balanced. Here are a few ways you can guard against the spirit of fear:

- Remember that the joy of the Lord is your strength. Make a decision to hold onto promises of God, no matter what things look like around you. His joy will carry you through anything!
- Guard your heart. Your emotions can set off a firestorm, if they're not managed properly. Set your heart to be in a place of peace and

reliance on the Word of God. Express your emotions in the right way, and don't allow fear to dictate anything to you.

• Guard your mind. Your thinking is the key to your stability in fearful times. Philippians 4:8 tells us where to focus our thoughts: "Whatever things are true, whatever things are noble, whatever things are just, whatever things are pure, whatever things are lovely, whatever things are of good report, if there is any virtue and if there is anything praiseworthy—meditate on these things." When you control your thoughts, the enemy cannot invade your imagination with terror or fear.

14

Inventions and Medical Advances

But you, Daniel, shut up the words, and seal the book until the time of the end; many shall run to and fro, and knowledge shall increase.

Daniel 12:4

I had traveled to Jordan, Lebanon, and a group of other countries on a ministry trip. I was in the desert. It was my first time in several of these nations. I remember how strikingly clean and sterile the buildings were in Jordan and some other desert countries. They were modern and beautiful, yet it seemed like being in the middle of nowhere. The walls were covered in glass windows. I looked out, and as far as I could see, sand dunes—mountains and mountains of sand.

I felt as if I were in a movie. In the distance, I could hear the sound of Arabic singing coming from the minarets. It echoed in my ears as it seemed constant for a while. The voice of a person signing in prayer to his god would be low, and then crescendo in this interesting way. I saw many people's dedication, which moved me even more to evangelize and pray for them to come to Christ.

After I reached my destination, at some point I was taken to a private prophetic meeting. Due to the jetlag from all the travel I was doing, the timeline is a bit meshed together in my head. But I know I made it to the meeting. After a nice meal, those in the group chatted and we shared about how God was moving.

I was then taken to another room. The person there began to tell me they had brought me there so I might pray and prophesy over some very important blueprints. I was caught off guard. The Lord had not revealed that to me. I thought to myself, *What am I supposed to do? I don't understand why they would want me to do that.*

These were important people who had a relationship with Jesus, so I listened. They unraveled this huge roll of plans that looked like a foreign language to me. I stared at the plans, trying to understand them. It was like trying to read Mandarin, a language that I love but don't know how to speak or understand.

Yet when I looked at the plans, something leaped in my spirit. I began to pray and release the word of the Lord in great detail regarding what would come about with this key invention. Later, I would find out that God moved and fulfilled that word. I found out that they had brought me the plans for a major invention developed by top inventors and engineers in that particular country. Their government wanted to use the invention, but also sell it to another country for its military. The technology that they had me pray over was so innovative that it would be a game changer and completely disrupt industries if the average person were to get his or her hands on it. I was sworn to secrecy and asked not to share the details of it, and I have not. It was top secret.

At the moment that I prayed and gave the word of the Lord, I believe that the Spirit of God came upon me with an anointing for inventions and ideas. God told me that this is what's supposed to be upon the Church. He told me that in future days ahead, He would pour out innovation, inventions, and God ideas that would radically change the way we do life.

Those in the secular world who don't know Christ only receive these great ideas when people in the Body of Christ are unprepared or are not in a position to receive them and do something about it. Think about how many times you got an idea for an invention, had a dream about a product, or thought of something new that needed to be on the market. You may have forgotten about it, and then months or years later you see the product pop up on a commercial or in a store. Then you think, *That was my invention!* But you never did anything with it.

Gone are the days of having that negative testimony. The days are here when believers will be the scientists, inventors, engineers, doctors, business leaders, and the like, who will put forth products that bring solutions to our broken world. As you read this, know that God may have given you an idea or invention to shift your family, community, or nation. Don't sit on it; do your research and get that product out. It's your time to start creating with your blueprints from heaven!

In spite of wicked agendas now operating in the world, a great day of visitation is upon us. This will be one of the greatest times for believers everywhere! There will be great medical advances and inventions that will propel us forward as a human race. God has shown me a glimpse of some of these groundbreaking innovations that will come in the future. But before I share those prophecies, I want to admonish you that *you, too, carry innovation and creativity.* I believe God wants to give you keen vision for the future so you will be able to help others with the love and compassion of Christ.

One of the many ways God inspires us to help others is through ideas. God ideas may come in the simple form of thoughts He places in your mind. These thoughts are powerful tools that have the potential to change and transform people and their lives forever. An invention, idea, or innovation can come through a thought that can impact your community and positively improve some of society's ills.

Proverbs 8:12 (KJV) says, "I wisdom dwell with prudence, and find out knowledge of witty inventions." That phrase *witty inventions* comes from the Hebrew word *machashabah*, meaning purpose, device, plot (plan), and invention.[1] In the days ahead, heaven will be releasing building plans for the future. There will be strategies, devices, and ingenuity that will push the purpose of God in the earth. Witty inventions come from the Hebrew root word *zamam*, meaning "to have a thought, devise, plan, consider," and to "fix thought upon."[2] Here, God connects inventions to thoughts. For this reason, your renewed mind will be your greatest weapon and tool for advancing. God wants to use you to design products, invent new devices, and create new strategic plans, systems, and infrastructures that mirror His Kingdom.

A New Mind

Romans 12:2 tells us to "be transformed by the renewing of your mind, that you may prove what is that good and acceptable and perfect will of God." When we have the mind of Christ, we can release His perfect will in our world. His will is for healing, wholeness, wealth, mental stability, and so much more. You can experience that within yourself and release it to others simply by allowing Christ to take control of your thinking. You do this by fixing your mind on the Word of God and eschewing evil and those things that are not of Him.

> But now put away and rid yourselves [completely] of all these things: anger, rage, bad feeling toward others, curses and slander, and foulmouthed abuse and shameful utterances from your lips!
>
> Do not lie to one another, for you have stripped off the old (unregenerate) self with its evil practices,
>
> And have clothed yourselves with the new [spiritual self], which is [ever in the process of being] renewed and remolded into [fuller and more perfect knowledge upon] knowledge after the image (the likeness) of Him Who created it.
>
> Colossians 3:8–10 AMPC

This passage uses the terms *renewed* and *remolded*. Some dictionary definitions of the word *renew* include resuming or reestablishing something after an interruption, repeating an action, and giving fresh life or strength to something broken or worn out. When God renews your mind, He is doing all these things. He is replacing the pieces of your mental framework that have been broken, shattered by trauma, or worn out from just doing life.

The word *remolded* means changing or refashioning the structure, appearance, or character of something. When God renews and remolds your mind, He is doing an overhaul to your thinking and the very foundation of your belief system. When He remolds your mind, He is strengthening your integrity to operate righteously, and developing your character to deeply reflect His nature, essence, and likeness.

When your mind is transformed in this way through the Word of God and the working of the Holy Spirit, you become new. You become positioned to release inventions from heaven that the world has never seen. I believe there are solutions, plans, and inventions in the heavenly realm that are hovering over the earth, waiting for someone with the mind of Christ to capture them, create them, and materialize them. You are that person with the mind of Christ, who is about to possess the inventions of heaven and see them exist in the earth. Ahead are a few prophecies and visions about soon-coming advancements.

Planes and the aviation industry vision

The aviation industry is about to go through a major overhaul. Their systems will begin to implode because they have become so outdated in America and other nations. You will see mishaps, near accidents, and some actual accidents with planes due to a crumbling infrastructure in some areas. During that time, intercessors must pray against collisions, crashes, and equipment malfunctions. The Lord has shown me that these disasters are what the enemy wants to cause in the aviation industry. If we pray, we can stop some of these severe things from occurring.

After that, aviation technology that has been suppressed will skyrocket. New types of planes will emerge that travel at incredibly high speeds. They will break the sound barrier, but somehow, I see in this prophetic vision that these engineers will develop technology to muffle the booming sounds that would cause issues. These flights will be massive, and you won't be able to feel the turbulence when you are in the sky. It will feel as if you are on the ground. These will be like massive sky ships. They will begin to adapt some of the amenities that you see and experience on cruise ships and in luxury hotels. As farfetched as this may seem, this vision looked like something off a *Star Trek* episode.

Prophecy of medical advancements

The medical field globally will find itself in crisis, due to new diseases and viruses that will continually plague the population. Yet innovation will arise from key people and places. You will see many of the common diseases that people have battled and suffered from become a thing of the past. Medications will come forth that have been around the whole time but have not been made available to the masses. These medications will be released and bring healing to what the medical field has often deemed incurable. That's right—I heard God say to me that cures will be developed for many of the incurable diseases in the world in the near future.

Through artificial intelligence, operations that were impossible will become possible. Some surgeries will become more precise, and the time will be shortened. The Lord said to me, *Because of the death, disease, and health challenges that have afflicted many, I'm sending a wave of healing to counter what the enemy has sent. Get ready to see healing on another level. This healing will come through doctors, new, more effective treatment methods, healing medicine, and yes, supernaturally into bodies. You will hear mystery cases of people who had incurable diseases being healed instantly. The medical field will marvel at and study them, but it will be My doing.*

Prophecy of cancer healed

The Spirit of the Lord revealed to me that many of the types of incurable cancers that we see today will be seen no more. I know that may catch you by surprise. You may think, *That's impossible!* But I want you to know that nothing is impossible for our God. I saw a vision of cancer patients being treated with a simple pill. In the same way that we take a pill for less threatening diseases, you will see some cancers being treated effectively. At that time, it will be headline news globally. People will marvel and ask, "How could this be?" But God says, *The world is coming into an era of healing and innovation. Get ready for it!*

I've shared this over the past few years: I saw two key innovators being raised up to annihilate certain cancers. In the vision, one was a Black woman. There is a technology she's developing where through a certain procedure cancer will be eliminated from the body. It won't be cut out with a regular incision or surgical knife; this operating device will use light technology to eradicate cancer. You will see this innovation be approved and widely accepted in the medical field in the years to come.

The other individual that I saw is a young Jewish man. He's a genius, and the Lord says, *He has already developed a cure.* We have not heard of it in this natural realm yet, but it's coming. You will see this brilliant doctor and innovator do what others have said is impossible.

Vision of pharmaceutical witchcraft exposed

The medical industry will come under the divine judgment of God in the days ahead. This will take place because of corruption, and even the poisoning of many through adverse medications known to cause harm, while the people behind such things have continued to make money. God showed me a great exposure coming to the medical industry that will shake things up. Several pharmaceutical companies will go belly-up and will be shut down due to their negligence and corruption. I saw altered medical trials and some data completely covered up so that these companies could bypass standards in order to make money. You will see back-to-back massive exposure on this hit major headline news. This will represent a signaling in the industry that great change is on the horizon.

The word witchcraft in the Greek language is the word *pharmakeia*. It shows up in Galatians 5:20 as one of the works of the flesh that will cause people not to inherit the Kingdom of God. That word *pharmakeia* means sorcery and witchcraft. It also means medication.[3] Not all medicine is bad, of course, but this word is speaking of that which controls, alters, manipulates, and adversely affects the mind, body, and soul. The word *pharmakeia* is also the root of the English word *pharmacy*. That's right—*witchcraft* and *pharmacy* are the same exact word. Again, many pharmacists do good work. Yet one of the biggest, boldest forms of sorcery operating in the world today is the pharmaceutical industry. The global pharmaceutical industry has grown massively over the past couple of decades. Pharma's worldwide revenue totaled 1.48 trillion U.S. dollars in its most recent yearly totals.[4] Witchcraft and the love of money go hand in hand.

Let me qualify all of this by saying that there are many good doctors, nurses, healthcare providers, and medical facilities. What I'm saying is not intended as any slight to them, but the Lord showed me that the entire industry as a whole is sick. Exposure and the judgment of the Lord will come to correct those things that have been out of order. This will not happen overnight, and yes, corruption will always hide in the cracks and crevasses of the world until the return of Christ. The hand of God, however, will judge and shake what can be shaken within that industry. You will see it manifest in the days ahead.

Because there is witchcraft operating through big pharma, you must be careful what you put into your body. Pray and ask the Lord before you take certain medications, vaccines, or treatments, and also read, research, and consult with a respected medical professional first. The Holy Spirit will give you discernment to know what to do. There are many amazing things we are about to see come through the medical industry. God will judge the witchcraft and sorcery at the same time.

PROPHETIC INTEL

Anointed doctors, nurses, healthcare professionals, scientists, innovators, leaders of industries, and more are being raised up for such a time as this. Groups of them are emerging that will have a solid biblical foundation, and the Holy Spirit will begin to speak to them. When viruses and diseases hit (some of which will be man-made), God will show these godly experts what to do. Some will dream of the compounds, mixtures, and antidotes needed. Some will have sudden ideas, and others through their research will stumble upon major medical breakthroughs.

God will give ingenuity and genius to those whom He has chosen. These will be prophetic professionals and specialists. They will partner with the Holy Spirit to see incurable diseases eliminated. The pharmaceutical industry will try to stop them because what they're doing will be a threat to the massive loads of money being made corruptly. It has displeased God that many in that industry have been profiting off making people sick. They have benefited from sickness and from the poisonous ingredients in the food. God has seen this, and He will bring exposure and great judgment.

Some of the professionals God is raising up in this area for good will be greatly persecuted and even fear for their lives. Nevertheless, the Lord will be using them to save lives and preserve a generation.

PART THREE

GOD'S KINGDOM ADVANCING

15

Back to Acts

And it shall come to pass in the last days, says God, that I will pour
out of My Spirit on all flesh . . .

Acts 2:17

The gospels are historical and spiritual accounts of the disciples and their
journey with Jesus Christ as He walked the earth. The synoptic gospels
are comprised of Matthew, Mark, and Luke. *Synoptic* comes from a Greek
word meaning having a common or general view. These books are similar
in accounts, historical views, and spiritual principles. The English Standard
Version Study Bible says this:

> The Gospels have a genre parallel in the ancient world that was called the
> bios. This was ancient biography. Rather than focus on physical description
> and tracing phycological thinking and personal development like modern
> biographies, a bios highlighted the key events that surrounded a person
> and his teaching.[1]

The synoptics generally follow the same structure, except that Matthew and Luke go into detailed genealogies connected to Israel's history.

Matthew 1:1 begins with the most significant genealogical information—the lineage of Christ. It reveals that He is the son of Abraham and the son of David.[2] Further, the synoptic gospels parallel the Old Testament story of Israel, and they provide a context and explanation of the historical relationship between God and His people. These gospels are written as biographies of Jesus Christ. They greatly detail His birth, life, ministry, and resurrection, with the exception of Mark, which is shorter and gives fewer details.

The book of Acts is similar to these gospels, but differs in one main area. It is the only New Testament book that tells of the ministry of the apostles.[3] Luke wrote the book of Acts as a continuation of the book of Luke. He juxtaposed the ministries of Paul and Peter as they mirrored the pattern of Jesus' earthly ministry. Early in Jesus' ministry, He healed a man who was crippled or paralyzed (see Mark 2:1–12). In the same manner, Peter healed a crippled man in Jerusalem (see Acts 3:1–11). Likewise, Paul healed a crippled man in Lystra (see Acts 14:8–10).

Further, Jesus raised Jairus's daughter from the dead (see Luke 8:40–42, 49–56). As Peter ventured into his ministry in Joppa, he raised Tabitha from the dead (see Acts 9:36–43). The same model is seen with Paul in Troas, where he raised Eutychus from the dead (see Acts 20:7–12).

Jesus encountered many devils and cast them out. The apostles continued in the same Holy Spirit power. In addition, Peter confronted Simon the sorcerer and released God's judgment upon him (see Acts 8:9–24). Paul confronted Elymas the sorcerer, and by God's judgment Elymas was stricken with blindness (see Acts 13:6–11).

These are a few of the many examples showing the pattern and continuation of Christ's ministry in the earth. The book of Acts is a book of patterns. God uses it as a prototype for how the Church should function, love people, and neutralize the ills of humanity until the return of Christ.

There are many significant occurrences in the book of Acts. Among them, Acts 2 details the most notable—the release and outpouring of the Holy Spirit. The Spirit was given on the Day of Pentecost as 120 Christians waited in the Upper Room (see verses 1–4). The gift of the Holy Spirit completely revolutionized the Church and changed the world. This began the expansion of the Church of Jesus Christ from Jerusalem throughout the world.

Another notable event is Paul's conversion, detailed in Acts 9. He was on the road to Damascus when Jesus appeared to him and knocked him off his donkey. This passage shows Christ revealing Himself to Paul and launching him into ministry. Paul's conversion experience affected the future history of the Church. He became a powerful apostle who carried the Gospel to the Gentiles. The apostle Paul had a heart for the Jews, but a ministry primarily to the Gentiles. He continued the ministry of Jesus and furthered Christ's message. His missionary approach was to go wherever the Spirit of God would lead him. His mission was to equip believers in the Christian Church and evangelize the lost. He would do these things at all costs, even at the expense of his own life. Throughout Paul's missionary journeys, he was imprisoned, beaten, stoned, and left for dead. Ultimately, he gave his life for the mission of Jesus Christ that he believed in.

The Church Is in Transition

The Church is in one of the greatest and most crucial transition periods that we've ever seen. Organizations are being deconstructed, and some are being completely dismantled. The vernacular language of the Church is also being overhauled as the Lord begins aligning our words back with the original language and principles of the Bible. He is giving fresh language to a Kingdom movement emerging in the earth.

Much of today's preaching has drifted away from Christ-centered ministry, toward entertainment and performance-based teaching. This kind of ministering bears no fruit and doesn't help people in the long run. But the Church is in transition! God is purifying pastors, ministers, and leaders. He is cleansing out the ambition and ego of prophets and apostles. He is healing and refocusing evangelists to reach the lost. Further, He is grounding and giving knowledge to teachers to rightly divide the Word of truth.

After the cleansing and cutting away, the Church at large will expand. This will be a long and grueling process on the threshing floor, separating the wheat from the tares. This process will lead to the refining, polishing, and new reformation of the Church.

The Church will come forth in a new power, as a remnant emerges stronger than ever before. The resulting expansion, revival, and harvest of souls will be like what we read about in the book of Acts. The Church was birthed in Jerusalem and from there spread all over the world.

Renaissance and Revival

In Acts, revival and passion for the things of God didn't start in a synagogue or church building. Revival started in homes, city streets, the marketplace, and the places where people frequently gathered. People encountered Jesus in their everyday life. In Western society, we've become so far removed from this concept that many now only allow God to move on a Sunday in church.

Church has become known as a religious institution. The word *institution* refers to an establishment that governs and holds its traditions. But what if I told you that the Church in the book of Acts was never a religious institution? It wasn't an institution founded on tradition. The institution that tried to stop the early Church movement was made up of the Pharisees and Sadducees. These were religious leaders who were well-versed in Torah (Scripture), yet they had no personal revelation of the Son of God. They followed the Law of Moses to the letter, yet they were void of the Holy Spirit.

Today, we don't hear of Pharisees or Sadducees in religious circles. In Western nations, there hasn't been an ongoing direct, violent persecution of the Church by its leaders. There has, however, been a slow decay of morality, sound doctrine, and Spirit-led preaching and demonstration, as well as a drifting away from Christ-centered ministry. When we see these things, a revival must come. Psalm 80:18–19 connects to the core message of the book of Acts: "Then we will not turn back from You; revive us, and we will call upon Your name. Restore us, O LORD God of hosts; cause Your face to shine, and we shall be saved!" Revive in this passage is the Hebrew word *chayah*. It is defined as bringing back to life, restoring to consciousness, or as a rebirth or renaissance.[4]

The word *renaissance* stands out to me in that definition. We use the term *renaissance* now to mean a period in history that occurred several hundred years ago:

The Renaissance was a period of "rebirth" in arts, science and culture, and is typically thought to have originated in Italy.

The Renaissance, which means "rebirth" in French, typically refers to a period in European history from A.D. 1400 to A.D. 1600. Many historians, however, assert that it started earlier or ended later, depending on the country. It bridged the periods of the Middle Ages and modern history, and, depending on the country, overlaps with the Early Modern, Elizabethan and Restoration periods.[5]

During the Renaissance, man-made religious practices were challenged, such as indulgences, bribery, and more. This influenced the Reformation, sparked by a German monk named Martin Luther when he wrote the "95 Theses" and nailed them to the door of the Castle Church in Wittenberg. In the same manner as there was a rebirth of the Church then, we are headed for a major overhaul now. Let me end this chapter with a couple of prophecies about some changes ahead for the Church:

Prophecy of a switch happening

God has said to me, *Things will not be as they appear.*

We will see another renaissance of the Church in the coming months and years. It will be sparked by what looks like a sudden decline of the Church. The Church's systems will come unhinged in many religious sectors. Church membership and the number of those professing to be Christians seemingly will decline in many Western nations. Headlines will say the Church age is over.

Some major leaders who have been looked to as pillars in the Church world will come down. Some will end their ministries in scandal, while others will suddenly be removed, or will no longer retain their relevance. It will seem as though the Church is in an unprecedented crisis.

The Spirit of the Lord has said to me, *At that time, you will see a switch begin to happen. Many corrupt religious institutions will crumble. What appears to be a crisis will be an opportunity for evangelism, revival, and an awakening of the remnant, the true Church. You will see radical conversions of those who are deemed the least likely. You will see prodigal sons and daughters have a true encounter with My Spirit. During what looks like a decline, the church model will begin to shift. For I am changing the face of the Church. The Church will return to a New Testament, book of Acts model.*

Not only did the Lord show me a revival and harvest of souls; I also saw this switch leading to a reformation of the organizational systems. Although it will be a painful and messy process, we are coming into a new Renaissance age of the Church. You will see a revival in eleven key areas of the Church. This new Renaissance age of the Church will include the revival of:

1. The gifts of the Spirit (operating at optimal level)
2. The art of prayer and fasting
3. Revival of sound doctrine
4. Pure prophetic ministry
5. Arts and liturgy
6. Prophetic science (believers who are experts in biology, physics, chemistry, and mathematics being trained by the Spirit)
7. Songs of deliverance, prophetic songs, and songs full of the Word
8. Revival of Christian business and industry leaders
9. Governmental apostolic voices
10. Evangelists who have a mandate for souls
11. Pastors who are equipped to care for the sheep

Prophecy of a gathering anointing

There will be a wave of revivals that begin to sweep across nations. These will not be man-made experiences with extensive preplanned programs. Many of these gatherings will be supernaturally orchestrated, and some will even be spontaneous.

There is a gathering anointing being released in the earth. God is pouring out His fresh oil on those who are being equipped to gather people of all backgrounds, cultures, and experiences. Key leaders will be raised up and positioned to champion new movements from the Lord. An anointing will be released to fill stadiums, arenas, sports fields, convention centers, and yes . . . even the streets. This will be for a season in America again, and in other nations.

After this season, there will come a scattering of modern-day missionaries, evangelists, and leaders into obscure, overlooked areas. A coming persecution against the Church will cause the Gospel to be taken into unchurched and unconventional areas. This will be one of the Church's finest hours.

PROPHETIC INTEL

Church growth exploded in the book of Acts. The message of the Gospel spread from Jerusalem to Antioch, to Judea, Samaria, and throughout the world. This gave way to great enlargement, but also to great conflict that actually helped the Church continue to thrive. Likewise, we as believers today will be faced with the challenge to grow collectively and develop as we advance the Kingdom of God. Here are some things you can do to get back to Acts:

- Embrace the inner working of the Holy Spirit. Allow the Spirit's power to stir within you. Allow the Holy Spirit to pray through you fervently to see God's will performed in your life and in the lives of those around you.
- Get back to the ministry of Jesus. Be Christ centered in all you do. This will cause you to develop a heart of serving and a deeper love for others.
- Take care of the widows and orphans (see Acts 6:1–3; James 1:27). This is what true, pure, and undefiled religion is. Give to the poor and to those who have not. This is the same as giving to the Lord Himself and will cause the blessings of God to flow back to you.
- Build a spiritual altar in your house—simply a place set aside where you can meet daily with God, and where you can pray and spend time in His Word and in worship. Make your house

a sanctuary and know that your body is the Temple of the Holy Spirit.

- Don't compromise your values, your character, or your biblical standard to fit in with the world. Embody and emulate the character and attributes of Jesus Christ.

16

The Remnant Church Rising

Count it all joy when you fall into various trials, knowing that the testing of your faith produces patience. But let patience have its perfect work, that you may be perfect and complete, lacking nothing.

James 1:2–4

Revelation 12 is a picture of the Church in times of tribulation. The pregnant woman represents the Church pregnant with the Kingdom of God:

And there appeared a great wonder in heaven; a woman clothed with the sun, and the moon under her feet, and upon her head a crown of twelve stars:

And she being with child cried, travailing in birth, and pained to be delivered.

And there appeared another wonder in heaven; and behold a great red dragon, having seven heads and ten horns, and seven crowns upon his heads.

And his tail drew the third part of the stars of heaven, and did cast them to the earth: and the dragon stood before the woman which was ready to be delivered, for to devour her child as soon as it was born.

And she brought forth a man child, who was to rule all nations with a rod of iron: and her child was caught up unto God, and to his throne.

And the woman fled into the wilderness, where she hath a place pre-pared of God, that they should feed her there a thousand two hundred and threescore days.

And there was war in heaven: Michael and his angels fought against the dragon; and the dragon fought and his angels,

And prevailed not; neither was their place found any more in heaven.

And the great dragon was cast out, that old serpent, called the Devil, and Satan, which deceiveth the whole world: he was cast out into the earth, and his angels were cast out with him.

Revelation 12:1–9 KJV

We can see from this passage that the woman and her baby—or the Church carrying the Kingdom—are under intense persecution. The persecution is so bad that she has to flee into the wilderness, which at the time of the writing was considered dangerous and deadly. The wilderness in this passage is not how we Westerners picture a wilderness. When the Bible speaks of the wilderness, it is most often referring to a desert place without much water or food, and with harsh and deadly conditions. The journey through the wilderness itself would have been a life-threatening ordeal.

Here we see a woman in transition. Scripture says she was travailing in birth. *Travail* is an intense prayer made by the Holy Spirit, through the human spirit, to bring to pass a prophetic promise. The word *travail* occurs thiery-one times in the Bible. It means pain, anguish, or suffering associated with childbirth. There's a strong connection between the words *travel* and *travail*. They both actually come from the Latin root word *trepalium*, which was an instrument of torture in the old world.[1] So when the woman was both travailing in birth and traveling into the wilderness, she was in a dangerous situation. And just like the woman, the Church is fighting to fully birth out the Kingdom of God in an era of global transi-tion. Like the woman, the Church is being persecuted and is in a potentially dangerous situation.

But Scripture says that "the earth helped the woman, and the earth opened its mouth and swallowed up the flood" (Revelation 12:16). As I said, the woman is the Church. The Church has been in transition, and we have stepped into a new era. We are shifting, traveling, and travailing, and the end result is God bringing forth the Kingdom of God. "For indeed," Jesus told us, "the kingdom of God is within you" (Luke 17:21). And just like the woman, the Church will be protected and sustained by what looks like the wilderness. There will come a day when the remnant Church will have to go underground. Governments will pass laws that make it illegal to preach the Gospel. But the *Ekklesia*, or the "called-out ones," are conditioned to survive persecution.

The Rise of the Pseudo-Church

As the remnant Church has been growing, there has been a pseudo-church rising at the same time. Just as the real Church is typified by a woman, so is the pseudo-church. We see this referenced in Revelation 17, where she is referred to as the whore of Babylon, drunk off lust. This pseudo-church is said to be the mother of prostitutes and the abominations of the earth (see verses 1–5). That lets us know that her messaging is both permissive and for sale. Her morality is not rooted in truth, but rather in what she can gain for herself.

The whore of Babylon is not only drunk off lust; she is also drunk off the blood of God's holy people (see Revelation 17:6). We often discuss the persecution of the Church from without, but we rarely talk about the persecution that seemingly comes from within. There is coming a time very soon—in fact, the time is here—when we in the Church will be persecuted for our stance on righteousness and holiness. This is why the Bible says in Mark 13:9 that we will not only be turned over to the courts, but will be "beaten in the synagogues." The word *churches* didn't exist to refer to Christian meeting places when Mark wrote his gospel, so he used the word *synagogues*, indicating persecution from within. The believers at the time still referred to themselves as being part of the same religion as the Jews.

Likewise in our day, we see that the modern pseudo-church will join with the world and declare that our stance for righteousness as Christians is hateful, antiquated, and not God's true intention. We saw the precursors of this in the hyper-grace movement that gained a lot of traction in the early 2000s. But it has since taken many names and faces, such as inclusionism or any other post-modern interpretation that focuses on experience over reason. These interpretations seek to change the image of God into mankind's, instead of us being transformed into the image of Christ.

Religion has always been a tool used to control people. The pseudo-church forms partnerships with leaders. She uses her influence to get support for these leaders, and in turn they yield their authority to this foul woman. The leaders then are mobilized to wage war against the Lamb, who is Head of the true Church. But the Lamb and His followers overcome!

This imagery of the whore of Babylon also shows a pseudo-church that has an outward presentation similar to the true Church, but its interests are drastically different. The pseudo-church desires to take for itself, appeal to the sensual nature, and gravitate to what feels good. She is often entangled in the affairs of this world. Not only has she been used to fortify natural kingdoms; she also teaches about human power more than divine power.

Because the pseudo-church operates in the fleshly nature so often, it's not uncommon for it to display an image of godliness, but be without real power. Often, there will be a strong divination in some of these pseudo-churches, where people will openly prognosticate against dissenters, and through fear these "prophecies" against people will come to pass. False signs and wonders will also occur that are widely reported, to give apparent credence to the pseudo-church's authority. There are almost always measures of control implemented through fear, anger, and greed, and these are usually upheld under the titles of "righteousness" and "hard work." And the works that are done give glory and credit back to the person, and not to Christ.

In contrast, the true Church has been admonished to stay sober and vigilant (see 1 Peter 5:8). As the true Church, we walk in the Spirit so that we don't fulfill the lust of the flesh (see Galatians 5:16). The true Church is not entangled in the affairs of this world (see 2 Timothy 2:4), because she has been commissioned to teach the Gospel of the Kingdom of God. True signs and wonders follow the true Church (see Mark 16:17–18). The true Church still believes in the supernatural power of the Holy Spirit. She gives to the foreigner, widow, orphan, and those in need. She speaks life and offers opportunities for repentance, restoration, and healing. The true Church is an image of a nurturing and protective mother who watchfully brings her children to maturity in Christ.

Jesus is at the center of everything in the true Church, for she knows that if He is lifted up, He will draw all people to Himself (see John 12:32). Love and holiness are the foundation for the true Church. We separate from the world and corruption, and we cry out to the Father that we want to be holy, as He is holy. The true Church exhibits the fruit of the Spirit, which is "love, joy, peace, longsuffering, gentleness, goodness, faith, meekness, temperance" (Galatians 5:22–23 KJV). She loves people and does not condemn them. She walks in humility, submitting to God and esteeming others higher than herself. And no, true believers are not expected to be perfect. The only example the Bible gives us of perfection is Jesus. And that's a way to encourage us that despite our shortcomings, there's still salvation and hope for us. We are only expected to bring our weaknesses to God, because His strength is made perfect in our weakness (see 2 Corinthians 12:1–10).

Coming Persecution of the Perfect Bride

The Church is known as the Bride of Christ in Scripture, an expressive picture that shows the intimate and close relationship between believers and Jesus Christ. In the days ahead, the remnant Church will rise with greater power, authority, and influence in the earth. This will come with a hefty price. The Church will endure greater persecution and tribulation. It will be a weeding out and a pruning season. Many in the Body of Christ will face challenges and obstacles that seem impossible, but the Lord will carry us through it all.

We believers will be strengthened in knowing that God is with us, no matter how hard the situation may seem. These trials will develop a greater maturity and endurance in God's people. James 1:2–5 states,

> My brethren, count it all joy when you fall into various trials, knowing that the testing of your faith produces patience. But let patience have its perfect work, that you may be perfect and complete, lacking nothing. If any of you lacks wisdom, let him ask of God, who gives to all liberally and without reproach, and it will be given to him.

The joy of the Lord will be your strength when you find yourself facing difficult situations. God never promised us that we would not have to go through difficulties, but He did promise to use those for our good. When you find yourself going through hardship, rejoice! I know it might seem hard to do when your emotions are entangled with life's challenges. It might not make sense to your natural logic. Why would you rejoice in hard times? Yet when you learn to praise God through all things, He will do one of two things: Either He will change your situation while you praise Him, or He will change you while you're going through that trial. Either way, it works out for your good.

Trials have a way of maturing you and growing you up. Sometimes they are unavoidable because they are testing your faith. As James 1:3-4 explains, the testing of your faith produces *patience*. That word in the Greek language means consistency. Tests cause you to develop a stability in God where you must rely on Him. The more you're tested, the more your faith becomes consistent. The more your faith becomes consistent, the more you become complete, whole, and mature in Christ. The Word of God promises that through this process, you won't lack anything. There will be nothing broken and nothing missing from your life. James 1:5 goes on to tell us that if we lack any wisdom while going through difficult trials, all we need to do is ask God, and He is so faithful that He will give it to us freely. In other words, the Church is in an open-book test. We are being tested, but the ultimate Teacher, called the Holy Spirit, is there to give us all the answers and to help us through it.

The Bride of Christ in our day is going through another process of maturing in the things of God. You will see much of the division, infighting, and petty differences in the Church begin to fall away as we come into the unity of the faith. The days ahead will be a glorious time for the Church. There are many prognosticating the global Church's demise, but this is a lie from the pit of hell! The Church will rise in greater victory and unity in the days ahead. As a believer in the Lord Jesus Christ, you will be strengthened in your inner man. Your spirit will be renewed and rejuvenated. There are so many great things the Body of Christ has to look forward to, so many great promises to be fulfilled, so many victories, and so many great works to do.

Intensifying Gifts of the Spirit

In the days ahead, you will see an emphasis placed again on spiritual gifts, along with godly character. In previous years, many have sought to operate in a spiritual gift, but with no character. The character of God, also known as the fruit of the Spirit we just saw in Galatians 5, is the foundation for operating in the gifts of the Spirit in the right manner.

The apostle Paul makes it known that there is a variety of gifts that the Holy Spirit distributes to a variety of people:

> Now there are distinctive varieties and distributions of endowments (gifts, extraordinary powers distinguishing certain Christians, due to the power of divine grace operating in their souls by the Holy Spirit) and they vary, but the [Holy] Spirit remains the same.
>
> 1 Corinthians 12:4 AMPC

Although many scholars and preachers have tried to place an exact number on the gifts of the Spirit, here Paul makes it known that there are a variety. God's gifts cannot be contained or confined by the human mind, for the gifts of God are endless. His Word makes it clear that His ways are past finding out, and His wonders are without number (see Job 9:10). Paul lists some of gifts in 1 Corinthians 12:8–10. These gifts can be categorized by their functions. Let's look at three categories of three gifts each. There are the *revelatory gifts*, which include the word of wisdom, the word of knowledge, and the discerning of spirits. There are the *vocal gifts*, which include prophecy, diverse kinds of tongues, and the interpretation of tongues. Then there are the *power gifts*, which encompass faith, gifts of healing, and the working of miracles.

Revelatory gifts

The gifts of revelation unmask hidden truths and secret knowledge. These gifts are given to combat the age-old challenge for humanity called ignorance, which hides in the recesses of the mind. God makes it clear that He would *not* have us be ignorant even concerning spiritual gifts (see 1 Corinthians 12:1). Ignorance simply means that "you don't know." Revelation gifts are able to uncover what you don't know, mobilizing you to make right decisions, avoid unnecessary problems, and live a successful life.

1. Word of wisdom—This gift provides divine solutions for practical matters. The use of this gift always comes with a set of instructions. The

Spirit's instructions will tell an individual what to do to resolve a problem. When a true word of wisdom is given, if the instructions are heeded, then the problem will be eliminated. This is contingent upon the individual following the God-given instructions. In my ministry, I have seen this gift used very strongly in financial matters, relational matters, and even matters of health.

2. *Word of knowledge*—This is the second gift the apostle Paul mentions in his list. The word *knowledge* comes from the Greek word *gnosis*, meaning divine intelligence and understanding.[2] *Divine* simply means that the intelligence and understanding come from God. The Holy Spirit will utilize this gift to reveal information about a person, group of people, or situation. The gift's purpose will be to bring salvation, healing, or deliverance. It can also be used to build someone's faith. It is a sign to unbelievers that God exists and cares about every detail of their lives.

3. *Discerning of spirits*—To *discern* is to perceive or recognize something. The discerning of spirits is the ability to perceive or recognize what spirit is in operation in a person or situation. It's important to know what spirit is influencing individuals whom you encounter. A person's outward appearance may be deceiving, but a wise believer desires to know what lies within the person's heart. The Greek word for *discern* is *diakrisis*, which means a distinguishing or judging.[3] This gift allows those who have it to know the difference between what's pure and what's contaminated, the difference between what's good and what's evil.

Vocal gifts

Vocal gifts primarily require hearing or receiving inspiration from God and speaking it forth. These gifts are not fully operative without speaking or communicating. Prophets are known as the oracles of God because they stand in place as God's mouthpiece. Vocal gifts require public speaking, and these three gifts are like God's amplifiers. For this reason, it takes boldness and courage to stand and declare the words of the Lord.

4. *Prophecy*—This gift is essential to the office of a prophet, although it's not always confined to a believer holding that office. The gift of prophecy is

the privilege to foresee and foretell the future. Prophecy means a discourse emanating from divine inspiration. The purpose of prophecy is to reveal the heart and mind of God for His people. Prophecy will also reveal the future of humankind and God's plans for creation. The mysteries of God are revealed through prophecy.

5. *Diverse kinds of tongues*—Speaking in other tongues is a gift that has brought much controversy in the Body of Christ. However, the apostle Paul explains that there are tongues unknown to man. He also reveals that there are a wide variety of heavenly languages. He is speaking of spiritual languages that cannot be figured out by the natural human mind. This gift of divine communication can strengthen and encourage people's spirits and release prophecy.

6. *Interpretation of tongues*—Because unknown tongues can release prophecy, there's a need for the gift of interpretation. This gift is the ability to interpret what someone is saying in a heavenly language. Prophetic tongues have no meaning to a congregation if the people don't understand what's being said. The gift of interpretation brings clarity by releasing the words of prophecy in our earthly languages.

Power gifts

Power gifts demonstrate the supernatural ability of God. It is the power of God that makes you *able* to do what you couldn't do before. The power gifts are designed to transmit God's authority and capability to humankind. Signs and wonders are the result when these power gifts operate by the Spirit of God.

7. *Faith*—The gift of faith is a supernatural ability to believe God for the impossible. This gift often works in conjunction with the other power gifts. When the gift of faith is in operation, it causes supernatural occurrences to take place. True prophets have to walk in a realm of supernatural faith in order to do and say the things that God commands. The gift of faith is entirely different from the fruit of faith. Every believer has the fruit of faith, which is needed in order to receive salvation. However, everybody does not have the gift of faith to believe God for the impossible. The gift of faith is activated in challenging situations.

8. *Gifts of healing*—When speaking of this gift, Paul says *gifts of healing* plural. This indicates that there is more than one gift of healing. These gifts are multifaceted and comprehensive. This endowment manifests itself in a variety of ways to heal or take away sickness and infirmity. In the Scriptures, you see that at times Jesus commanded healing to take place and people were healed. At other times, He touched people and they were healed. Then there were times when He used unusual methods to bring healing, like spitting in the dirt and placing the mud on a man's eyes, which were then healed. Jesus is the prime example of someone utilizing the gifts of healing.

9. *Working of miracles*—A miracle is something that goes against the natural order of things or laws that govern our world. The laws of the spirit world are vastly different from this natural world. When a miracle occurs, it's the superimposition of spiritual laws over natural laws. The first miracle Jesus did, according to Scripture, was turning water into wine (see John 2:1–11). According to the laws governing our natural world, there is no way possible that water can become wine. In God's world, however, it is possible. Most people confuse miracles and healings, but they are very different. Another miracle in the Bible is where the prophet Elisha caused the axe head to swim (see 2 Kings 6:1–7). There is no way that iron can float, according to this world's natural laws. In order for that to happen, the molecular structure of the axe head had to change. In the spirit world, such things are possible.

Souls Coming into the Kingdom

The gifts of the Spirit will be activated with healings, signs, and wonders as a demonstration of God's power to reach the lost. The remnant Church will be filled with evangelists. No, all may not stand in that spiritual office, but we will all do the work of an evangelist. The heart of God is souls. Jesus came to save those who are lost. This will be the mission of the remnant in this new era.

The Church won't be focused on programs, agendas, and just doing conferences to do them, as we have seen in times past. The day is here when God's people will go into every system, industry, community, and street to share the saving message of the Gospel. People will see that there's something different about you and want to know what it is. You will be the sign and the wonder to testify of Christ. Isaiah 8:18 reveals that God's people are "for signs and wonders." You are called to show forth the glory of the Lord. Others will see your life as a testimony of what God can do for them. This is also the reason why God will allow you to go through—or should I say grow through?—some trials in front of others. This will be so they can watch Him deliver you.

A flood of souls will come into the Kingdom of God. Many who have been overlooked, rejected, and even hurt by some in the Church are coming in. We as a Body of Christ must be ready for them. We can't look upon them in harsh judgement, or with rejection. We must embrace them as part of the household of faith. They will come in looking very different from you, dressing very differently than you, but their hearts will be after God. Their praise and worship will be pure. Some will say they are misfits. Those who operate in a spirit of false religion will be appalled because these newcomers don't look like Christians. But God does not judge based on the outward appearance; He judges the heart of a person (see 1 Samuel 16:7).

Believers must be prepared to embrace these new Christians when they come in. Churches must be prepared to disciple them and not push them away. Their praise will be raw and authentic. This is the new breed that will come with a fire in their hearts and a boldness to dismantle the kingdom of darkness.

PROPHETIC INTEL

The Church of the Lord Jesus Christ is on the move and will increase in strength. The Church is the most powerful entity on the face of the earth. God will demonstrate His power through the Church, but she will also go through much tribulation and persecution. The Bible is clear that persecution and tribulation are part of the Christian experience. We cannot escape persecution; it's part of the assignment. There are benefits, however, to tribulation and persecution. Here are some takeaways to help you focus on God's plan in the midst of difficulty:

- Tribulation produces patience and increases your faith.
- Persecution comes to those who live for God. If you were not a threat to the enemy's kingdom, he would not try to oppose you.
- Tribulation brings in you a greater glory. This means that the transformative power of God increases on the inside of you exponentially. Think of trials as a gateway to spiritual promotion.
- Each time the children of Israel were afflicted, they grew and multiplied. In the same manner, affliction will cause God's people today to rise and soar.
- Opposition is a propeller. The more the enemy buffets you, the more you will advance and progress.

Remember these key points as you are rising and soaring in the things of God. If you are part of the Body of Christ, then you are part of the remnant and this is your time.

17

A Prophetic Generation

Your Sons and Daughters Will Prophesy

And it shall come to pass in the last days, says God, that I will pour out
of My Spirit on all flesh; your sons and your daughters shall prophesy,
your young men shall see visions, your old men shall dream dreams.

Acts 2:17

What an exciting time to be part of the Body of Christ! I believe that the
Body of Christ is entering the day of the *next generation*. This is a time
where the up-and-coming generation of the world will begin to emerge
with a passion and a zeal for the things of God. Now, I understand that
not everyone will be part of this emergence, but there are chosen people
whom God will use to usher in a new move of His Spirit. This remnant
of people will arise with a uniquely distinctive sound in the earth. A new
breed of warrior is coming forth right now!

The Bible informs us that God chose the young because they are strong
(see 1 John 2:14). It's this strength that will impact the nations of the
world. I believe that in these last days, God is kindling a fire in His people,

particularly in His emerging generation. He is raising up young adults who will be a flame of fire in the earth.

But why has God decided to kindle a fire? Take an insightful look at the Scriptures and you will be able to understand what's taking place in the earth: "And the barbarous people shewed us no little kindness: for they kindled a fire, and received us every one, because of the present rain, and because of the cold" (Acts 28:2 KJV). In this passage, Paul was on a journey where he was shipwrecked and experienced incredible challenges. He finds himself on an island called Malta. He refers to the people as barbaric, yet they still received them. A simple fire was started as a welcome. I believe this is a prophetic symbol of what we will see in the days ahead. A fire is about to be started that will draw people together. Those who would be considered rejects will open up to the message of Jesus.

The fire on Malta didn't only welcome the people; it attracted a viper as well. The viper bit Paul and latched on (see Acts 28:3–6). Everyone around who witnessed it thought Paul would die and that it must be the judgment of God for past sins. But Paul didn't die. The fire that drew the serpent also destroyed it. Paul remembered his promise from God, and he shook the serpent off into the fire.

The viper is a very cunning predator. Vipers hunt based on heat signatures. They go after would-be prey that is warmer than the surroundings. Heat-based hunting makes the viper proficient at hunting at night. They suddenly strike their victim, and their venom immobilizes the target. Once the venom is inside, it courses through the victim, causing inflammation and paralysis, and shutting down vital organs. The venom targets the heart, respiratory system, and kidneys first. The heart not only pumps blood, but is an analogy the Bible uses to signify the believers' love. The respiratory system represents the believers' ability to persist and keep going in the faith. The kidney represents the believers' ability to keep their "blood," which is Christ's DNA in them, pure from all the toxins in this world, such as hate, greed, lust, etc. And just like this viper targeting Paul in Acts 28:3, there are viper spirits targeting those who are on fire for God. They track the heat and movement and wait for their moment to strike. But like Paul, we must have a passion and fire so strong that we just shake off the attack and let the fire of God consume it. Passion, hunger, and being on fire for

God are going to be key for this generation in defeating the demonic spirits coming after them.

A fire was kindled on Malta because it was needed for the shipwreck's survivors as a result of the rain and cold. It's interesting that the Scripture says "barbarous people" kindled the fire. The word *barbarous* means "uncivilized; wild; savage; crude."[1] Barbarous also means "not conforming to classical standards or accepted usage, as language."[2] God therefore allowed a people who were savage, nonconforming, and uncivilized to kindle a fire that would receive everyone. I think this is very prophetic in nature. God is allowing a generation that has been called uncivilized and nonconforming to start a fire big enough to draw everyone. The generation that has been called rebellious, out of control, and even cursed is being delivered to bring about reformation, revival, and change to this world.

Presently, Satan has been raining down his deceptions and perversions in the earth, therefore causing the hearts of many to wax cold toward God. And if that's not reason for a fire to be kindled by the Holy Spirit, then what is? Sadly, not all in the emerging generation will be saved, but I strongly believe that there is a remnant of emerging believers, the previous generation's sons and daughters, who are about to be raised up for the times we are in and show forth the glory of God. God has called and selected a chosen people. If you know that you are part of that remnant, then allow a fire to come alive in you from the spiritual knowledge and instructional impartation revealed in this chapter.

Fire in the Next Generation

We talked in chapter 8 about how fire is a very unique element, completely different from the other three. We saw that although earth, water, and air are all forms of matter made up of atoms, fire is not matter at all. It is the visible, tangible side effect of matter changing form. It is one part of a chemical reaction. I want to decree to you prophetically that as it is in the natural, so it is in the spiritual. Fire only occurs as a side effect of matter (something that occupies space) changing forms. God is kindling a fire in this next generation. In the spirit, there's a reformation or a "re-forming" taking place in them. This next generation—or matter, metaphorically speaking—is changing form and resulting in a combustion known to us as fire. It's a chemical reaction signifying the revolution that is taking place in the spirit realm.

Typically, a fire occurs from a chemical reaction between oxygen in the atmosphere and some sort of fuel (for example, wood or gasoline). Of course, gasoline and wood don't spontaneously catch on fire just because they're surrounded by oxygen in the atmosphere. For a combustion reaction to occur successfully, *you* have to heat the fuel to its ignition temperature. Spiritually, this tells me that God is kindling the fire, but you also have a role to play in this spiritual reaction taking place. In other words, *you* control the ignition temperature. It's your role as a participant in this move of God to allow the Holy Spirit to take you as far as He wants you to go. What I mean by this is, don't diminish the size of the flame God is burning in you.

Luke 11:33 (KJV) states, "No man, when he hath lighted a candle, putteth it in a secret place, neither under a bushel, but on a candlestick, that they which come in may see the light." This particular Scripture indicates to us that the purpose of a candle being lit is so that others might see it. I want to let you know that the purpose of God lighting a fire in you is so that others may see it. This verse also says no man puts a candle in a secret place. Many times, as young people that's exactly what happens. God starts ministering to you and moving in your spirit, but you try to hide it so no one else can see it. The other part of the verse says no man puts a candle under a bushel. A bushel is a stack or a heap of something. When the Holy Spirit begins to kindle a fire in you, sometimes you may try to suffocate the fire. But I want to encourage you, don't hide or suffocate the fire. Let it burn in your spirit.

Someone who is not part of the remnant God has handpicked and selected may think that there is no last-day move of God. Someone who is religious and doesn't have a relationship with God may think that the next generation is completely lost and far from Him. However, I beg to differ. The Bible speaks clearly and informatively of the last-day move, even concerning this emerging generation. The "last-day move" is a reformation and revolution of the next generation. It signifies a great shifting in the earth. It also indicates a new demonstration of God's unlimited power. The last-day move of God is when the end-time sons and daughters of God take their rightful places and walk in the unlimited power of God. Someone may also be deceived into thinking that we have already experienced the last-day move of God, but if we're not seeing God move and demonstrate His power more greatly than He did in the book of Acts, then we're not experiencing the last-day move. All we're experiencing is hype and no real power! Jesus said that we, the sons and daughters of God, would do greater works than the ones we saw Him do.

Take a more in-depth look at how God wants to use young people powerfully today: "And it shall come to pass in the last days, says God, that I will pour out of My Spirit on all flesh; your sons and your daughters shall prophesy, your young men shall see visions, your old men shall dream dreams" (Acts 2:17). One significant phrase God uses is "*I will pour out of My Spirit on all flesh.*" That denotes that this last-day move isn't just going to be with Christians. This demonstration of God's power will be poured *upon all.* Teenagers, young adults, and people of all ages can take part in what God is going to do. Why? Because there are no age requirements on whom God can and will use in the earth. There are also no denominational or religious requirements. God said that He would pour out His Spirit *upon all.* Therefore, he who has an ear, let him hear what the Spirit of the Lord is saying: God does not care about your age, religion, ethnicity, or any other limit imposed by mankind. This is the simple message God wants the world to hear: Mankind's limitations cannot stop the move of the Spirit. God is just looking for a people who have a heart for Him. He wants people who will devote themselves to Him.

There are many people in this world who say they know and love God, but there are not many who will give God their full attention. People are wrapped up and tied up in the pleasures of this world and have forgotten their first love. I adjure you today to turn to God like never before and forsake those things that will pass away. Set your affections on the things that are above. Seek after God with all your heart. Make God first! No matter what your age, when you put God first and surrender to Him, then He will use you.

You must realize that God always wants to use those who make themselves available to Him. Look at the life story of Jeremiah. In the first chapter of the book of Jeremiah, God told him, "I have this day set you over the nations and over the kingdoms" (verse 10). When God spoke those few but impacting words to him, they propelled him into another dimension. God repositioned Jeremiah! That's what is taking place right now all over the world. God is repositioning His people and placing them in seats of power.

When Jeremiah was repositioned, it activated the prophetic anointing on his life. From that point on, the fire of God was stirred up in him. The prophet states in Jeremiah 20:9, "But His word was in my heart like a burning fire shut up in my bones." These words are not just mere words on a page, but are kindling a fire in the hearts of those who will hear.

A Passionate, Persistent Press for God

One thing I'm finding to be true in my walk with Christ is that God is a rewarder of those who diligently seek Him. I find that the more I seek God, the more He is revealed to me. In order for believers young or old to be on fire for God, there must be a press deep within our soul. It's important that you seek after God with all your heart. He loves diligent seekers. Diligent seekers are those who will press toward the high calling (see Philippians 3:14). If you don't go after what you desire, then you will never find it. You must have a passionate, persistent press for God. The Bible states in Ecclesiastes 9:11, "The race is not to the swift." The race is given to those who will endure until the end. Let's look individually at *passion*, *persistence*, and *pressing in*, and see how each of these attributes helps us endure to the end and win.

Possessing passion

To be a diligent seeker, you must possess passion. To be passionate is to have an immense love or feeling for something or someone. Most people would associate love and emotion with the word *passion*. However, there's much more to the definition of this word. *Passion* comes from the Latin word *passio*, which means the sufferings of Jesus or a martyr.[3] The word *passion* denotes an intense emotion to suffer or endure. To be passionate is therefore your ability to love God so much that you will endure persecution for Him. *Suffer* means to endure or bear, and to stand.[4] Paul insists in 2 Timothy 2:12 (KJV) that "If we suffer, we shall also reign with him: if we deny him, he also will deny us." The word *suffer* in the Greek is *hupomeno*, and it means "to remain i.e. abide, not recede or flee," and "to endure, bear bravely."[5] It also means "to preserve: under misfortunes and trials to hold fast to one's faith in Christ."[6] In 2 Timothy 3:12 Paul states, "Yes, and all who desire to live godly in Christ Jesus will suffer persecution."

One word I want you to take note of in the Greek definition of *suffer* is the word *abide*. Let's take a look at the definition of this word. *Abide* means "to wait for" and "to accept without opposition or question."[7] It also means "to submit to; agree to," and "to remain steadfast or faithful to."[8] Now let's put all of this together. If we are passionate about God, then we will suffer for Him, submit to Him, and accept what He says without opposition or question. In John 15:7, Jesus says, "If you abide in Me, and My words abide in you, you will ask what you desire, and it shall be done for you." This is such a powerful verse! I'm sure you may have heard this before, but may not have realized that it has everything to do with suffering. Here, Jesus is saying in effect, "If you are passionate after Me, submit to Me, suffer with Me, and most of all, believe what I say without opposition or question, then you can ask what you will and it shall be done unto you."

Therefore, the key to being passionate is to endure and suffer with Christ. But remember that 2 Timothy 2:12 states that if you suffer with Him, you will reign with Him. The word *reign* means to have royal rule or authority. So suffering causes you to have authority with God and man.

Possessing persistency

The next attribute you must have as an on-fire believer is persistency. The word *persistent* comes from the verb *to persist*. *Persist* comes from the two Latin words *per* and *sistere*, "to (cause to) stand." When you put them together, they make the compound Latin word *persistere*, which means "to stand firm permanently."[9] God is raising up a generation that will stand for the things that He stands for. This will be a generation that will stand for righteousness, holiness, biblical values, and most of all, the Word of God.

In order to survive and successfully thrive in today's world, you have to be persistent. In order to stand as the sons and daughters of God, we have to be persistent. To be persistent further means persevering in spite of opposition, obstacles, and discouragement. It also means refusing to give up or let go.

The Scriptures show many great examples of people who were persistent. Think of all the great and wondrous things the New Testament believers saw and experienced in the book of Acts. The New Testament Church was full of people who wanted to see God move and sought after Him persistently. They were a people who gave their lives for the Gospel.

You might ask, "What makes you so sure that if I seek after God, I'm going to find Him?" The Bible says, "Blessed are those who hunger and thirst for righteousness, for they shall be filled" (Matthew 5:6). The Bible also says that "the kingdom of God is . . . righteousness and peace and joy in the Holy Spirit" (Romans 14:17). If you hunger after the Kingdom of God, you will find it (you will be filled). Many people are not being "full filled" because they are not seeking after righteousness. Many wonder why they feel empty and without purpose. But there is only One who can make you whole and fulfilled in life—God. When you seek God first, He will add everything else you need.

Pressing in and forward

In addition, the word *press* means "to act upon with steadily implied weight or force." It means "to hold closely, as in an embrace," and "to push forward."[10]

What are you acting upon? If you are acting upon the Word of God, this means that when you read the Word, you apply it and its instructions to your life. Pressing in means that you hold the Word of God closely so that nothing will be able to take it from you.

It is that press or drive for God's Word that will cause you to push forward continually. *Forward* means "directed toward a point in advance; moving ahead."[11] When you press into God, you will always be ahead of obstacles, circumstances, and situations. It is your press that will cause you to defy the odds, statistics, and limits that have been set for you by mankind.

Jacob's Passionate, Persistent Press

Taking a journey into the Old Testament, I ran into a man who possessed the characteristics of an individual with a "passionate, persistent press." That man is Jacob. He had made some mistakes in his life. He had endured great trials, and now he was in trouble again. Jacob was in need of God to deliver him out of the hand of his brother, Esau. So Jacob went on a quest for God. He cried out for God to help him.

Jacob was in dire need, and if God couldn't help him, no one could. Therefore, he pressed in for a blessing and an endowment from God:

> And Jacob was left alone; and there wrestled a man with him until the breaking of the day.
>
> And when he saw that he prevailed not against him, he touched the hollow of his thigh; and the hollow of Jacob's thigh was out of joint, as he wrestled with him.
>
> Genesis 32:24–25 KJV

From this Scripture, we understand that Jacob wrestled with a man, or more likely an angel. Whoever this wrestler was, he had to have something valuable that Jacob desperately desired. This angel in the form of a man had access to God. Jacob knew that this being could give him something or do something for him that would change his fate, change his destiny forever. Let's read on:

> And he said, Let me go, for day breaketh. And he said, I will not let thee go, except thou bless me.
>
> And he said unto him, What is thy name? And he said, Jacob.
>
> And he said, thy name shall be called no more Jacob, but Israel: for as a prince hast thou power with God and with men, and hast prevailed.
>
> Genesis 32:26–28 KJV

I have to stop right there! Let's backtrack: Jacob fought with this angel all night long, until the next morning. The angel had knocked his thigh out of joint, but oh no, that didn't stop Jacob's press! Although he was hurt, he continued to wrestle. Just like Jacob, you have to press in for God, although something may be physically or spiritually wrong with you. There may be several issues going wrong, but you must continue to press in. Something in your past may be haunting you. Someone in your past may have hurt you. Yet if you continue to press in for God, you will find Him.

It may have seemed as though Jacob wasn't getting anywhere in his wrestling match. Of course, Jacob was no real match for this angel in the form of a man. However, I think the angel took note of the persistence that this *desperate* Jacob had. I'm sure God took note of it as well. Eventually, Jacob's persistence paid off. He was thrust into a new dimension because he chose to press in and forward. No matter what you've gone through or may be going through, if you press forward, God will take you farther than you ever thought you would go.

To recap a little, these words from the angel/man propelled Jacob into another dimension: "for as a prince hast thou power with God and with men, and hast prevailed." This means that Jacob was elevated because he pushed through all that was opposing and prohibiting his endowment.

But wait, there is more! Genesis 32:30 tells us, "And Jacob called the name of the place Peniel: for I have seen God face to face, and my life is preserved." For Jacob, this was more than just a mere blessing or experience with God. It was a face-to-face encounter.

Also, do you understand what it means for God to change your name? *Name* in the Hebrew is the word *Shem*, and it's pronounced shame.[12] It means reputation. In other words, God took the shame out of Jacob's reputation with a name change to *Israel*. He ultimately changed Jacob's fate and destiny. And for someone who is reading this, God is changing your name. You may be ashamed of your past. You may feel as though you are a failure in many ways. But God says that this day, your name has changed! You no longer have shame attached to your name. From this day forward, you will walk with a new name (reputation).

Alive, or Dying on the Inside?

In the midst of all the blessings Jacob received, most importantly his life was preserved. He had pressed in for his life, and that's the essential need of all. Today, a massive amount of the Body of Christ is drying up. Many of the people look good on the outside, but on the inside there's no life in them. The breath of God no longer resides there. What about you? You may look good on the outside too, but how do you really look on the inside? This is the question every believer must ask: *Am I alive, but dying on the inside?*

There are many effects that follow the loss of spiritual life. The main effect is that a person begins to be content with the place he or she is in. That's one of the first symptoms you feel when the enemy chokes the spiritual life out of you—you become complacent. In English, *complacent* means smug and self-satisfied. A complacent person has become content within himself or herself, not content in God. Also, a person who was once ignited and fired up for God begins to lose his or her power. With the breath of God comes creative abilities and power. Without that life or breath of God, you have no power.

When you start to see signs like complacency and a lack of power or ability, know that you are in danger of death—a spiritual death, that is. Death is not extinction, but separation from God. Remember that when you lose life, you put out the fire. When a fire is deprived of oxygen, the key element that enables all humanity to live on the earth in this natural realm, that fire no longer burns. All that's left is the memory of how it used to be a flame, and what the fire once did. And no one wants to be a faded memory. You should want to be on the cutting-edge move of God.

How does a person know if he or she is on the cutting-edge move of God? You know because the Bible proclaims strongly in Daniel 11:32 that a people who know their God shall be strong and do great exploits! So, if you currently aren't demonstrating the power of God even through hard trials, then you're not on the cutting-edge move of God. You demonstrate the power of God through your everyday living. When people notice that there's something different about you and that you're not like everyone else, then you've demonstrated God's power through your character. It's important to demonstrate God's power in every area of your life. It's your pursuit after God that causes the fire of God to be maintained in your life. Always remember that the true pursuit of happiness is having a passionate, persistent press for God.

New Wine

As God is igniting His people, it's coming with an infilling of the Holy Spirit. The Body of Christ is to be emptied out of *self* and full of the *Spirit*, because He is our power. There has been a misconception in the Body of

Christ concerning being full of the Holy Spirit. It's not just the ability to speak in another language unknown to mankind. When you have the Holy Spirit, He is your guide, protector, friend, and instructor.

The Spirit also gives you supernatural power: "But you shall receive power when the Holy Spirit has come upon you; and you shall be witnesses to Me in Jerusalem, and in all Judea and Samaria, and to the end of the earth" (Acts 1:8). This Scripture amplifies our vision to see where our power comes from. It comes from the indwelling of the Spirit of God. When the Spirit fills you, you become a witness to those around you, for the Bible strongly declares that "the kingdom of God is not in word but in power" (1 Corinthians 4:20). And if we don't have the Spirit of God, which is our power, we are not God's children: "But you are not in the flesh but in the Spirit, if indeed the Spirit of God dwells in you. Now if anyone does not have the Spirit of Christ, he is not His" (Romans 8:9).

Acts 2 is a two-fold chapter in the Bible because not only does it stress the importance of being full of the Spirit, but also of receiving the "new wine." In Scripture, wine is symbolic of God's anointing and refreshing. The apostle Peter declared in this chapter of Acts that the believers were not drunk with alcohol, but were drunk with the Spirit of God (see verses 14–17). Therefore, "new wine" is symbolic of the new anointing or move of God.

As believers, we have to be prepared and ready in order to receive the "new wine" God is pouring out. We have to be prepared in order to receive the new anointing God desires to rain heavily in and upon His people. Many believers are afraid of something new because they've never experienced it before. Whether they realize it or not, new is necessary! As the Scriptures tell us, there was need for a New Testament because there was a better way. "But in fact the ministry Jesus has received is as superior to theirs as the covenant of which he is mediator is superior to the old one, since the new covenant is established on better promises" (Hebrews 8:6 NIV).

There was an imperfection or flaw found in the old way the people of God used to do things. They used to sacrifice animals to the Lord. Now Jesus is the ultimate sacrifice, and the old things have passed away.

No man putteth a piece of new cloth unto an old garment, for that which is put in to fill it up taketh from the garment, and the rent is made worse.

Neither do men put new wine into old bottles: else the bottles break and the wine runneth out, and the bottles perish: but they put new wine into new bottles, and both are preserved.

Matthew 9:16–17 KJV

God wishes for His people to carry the new wine of the anointing and not the old. In order for us to carry the new wine, we must be prepared. God will not put new wine into old bottles, so we must understand the imperativeness of allowing God to prepare us to carry the new anointing. If we are not prepared and made ready to carry the new wine of the Spirit, then we will break and perish, just as the old bottles that were not prepared to carry the new wine.

You will not embrace the new move of God if you are not properly prepared and made into a "new bottle." A bottle is simply a vessel used for carrying a liquid. That's basically who we are as Christians. We are vessels that carry the Holy Spirit. Remember, it's important for you to be part of what God is doing now and not be stuck in the old move of God. Any Christian can tell what an old move consisted of, but not many will be part of what God is doing now in the earth. Keep in mind, and never forget, that it's easy to be full of the Spirit, but it's hard to be empty. In order to be full, you first must be totally emptied out of everything else. You can't be empty if you're not yielded to the Father. To empty out and yield to God takes something that not many people, let alone emerging generations, want to do—be completely sold out to God.

Yielded Vessel

The Lord is actively seeking a yielded vessel. He has so much He wants to do in the earth, and *through* His earth—you and me. It's important to understand that *we* are God's earth. According to the Word of God, we were made from the dust of the earth (Genesis 2:7). There are miracles, signs, and wonders that the Lord wants to demonstrate, but He needs a body to use. Not just anybody, but one that is yielded and humble before the Lord.

We must ask ourselves, *What must I do to be that yielded vessel of the Lord?* First of all, to be completely servile before the Lord will require you to give up some things that your flesh is unwilling to let go of. God is not a respecter of persons, and He will use anyone who is totally sold out to Him. Yet humility and timidity are often confused. Just because a person is quiet and solitary does not mean that he or she is humble or yielded to the Lord. False humility means that you show the persona of being humble, but on the inside you have wrong motives. True humility means that you obey the Lord's instructions and your heart is sincere before Him. Humility means that you are completely humble before the Lord, and there is no pride in you.

To be a yielded vessel, you must die to the flesh and be alive unto righteousness. When you destroy the deeds of the flesh and walk in the Spirit, you can be most effectively used of God. There is just one massive problem: There are not many people who are willing to give up their bodies as Jesus gave His up to be crucified for the sake of others! You must endeavor and be willing to deny yourself, as Jesus told His disciples in Matthew 16:24–26:

> If anyone desires to come after Me, let him deny himself, and take up his cross, and follow Me. For whoever desires to save his life will lose it, but whoever loses his life for My sake will find it. For what profit is it to a man if he gains the whole world, and loses his own soul? Or what will a man give in exchange for his soul?

This is a powerful passage of Scripture. It compels us to lay down our lives for the sake of the Gospel. If we as sons and daughters of God would lay down our lives for the sake of Christ, we would find life. I am continually finding that when I made the decision to give up my life, which consisted of giving up my will, I became a terror and threat to the enemy.

The Bible says that Jesus laid His life down; no man took it from Him (see John 10:17–18). If you look at Jesus, when He made the decision to give up His life, God set Him on the right hand of the Father in a "high place." A high place is a place of territorial rule, a place of absolute dominion and authority with God and men. When as a young believer you come to the ultimate conclusion that you are going to give up your life and deny yourself, God will set you in a "high place" too. That means you are seated in heavenly places with Christ, far above enemies, challenges, and the problems that you face here on earth (see Ephesians 2:4–6).

Giving up your life and denying yourself is not a one-time thing, however. You must continually yield to the Lord. Since we have talked about the urgency of being full with the Spirit, you can better understand what 1 Corinthians 6:19–20 tells us:

> Or do you not know that your body is the temple of the Holy Spirit who is in you, whom you have from God, and you are not your own? For you were bought at a price; therefore glorify God in your body and in your spirit, which are God's.

Understand that you are not your own. Jesus paid a price—a very expensive price—for you on the cross with His own flesh and blood. Now because you are not your own, God is requiring some things of you. He has need of you in this last-day move. But He can only use you if you are yielded, humble, and submitted under Him. So I pose these questions to you: Will you be a yielded vessel and allow God to use you? Or will you be like some and choose the things of the world over spiritual life?

Remember, even the earth is yearning for yielded vessels to arise as the true sons and daughters of God in the earth. Remember that yielding to God and killing your flesh is not just a one-time thing, but is a continual daily process. As long as you live, you will always have to deny yourself daily. Yet when you do that, you will be prepared to be filled with the new wine and will become even more of a terror and threat to the enemy.

An Unprecedented Manifestation

There will be a demonstration of the power of God in this last-day move like we have never seen before. This unprecedented manifestation will come through His sons and daughters. The true end-time sons and daughters of God will arise with boldness out of obscurity and show forth the matchless power of God!

I believe sincerely that the glory of God will be shown forth in the end-time sons and daughters of God. Romans 8:18–19 (KJV) says that the actual earth is awaiting this manifestation: "For I reckon that the sufferings of this present time are not worthy to be compared with the glory which shall be revealed in us. For the earnest expectation of the creature [earth] waiteth for the manifestation of the sons of God." A manifestation is something demonstrated or expressed in a revealing manner. As another translation puts verse 19, "the earnest expectation of the creation eagerly waits for the revealing of the sons of God" (NKJV). His true sons and daughters will take part in this revelation.

How do you know if you are a true son or daughter of God? Romans 8:14 provides insight on how you can tell if you have the traits of a true child of God, or if you are someone who lacks a heavenly Father: "For as many as are led by the Spirit of God, these are sons of God."

Those who are not led by the Spirit are not true children of God. You can be in church every Sunday. You can even preach and prophesy. But if you are not led by the Holy Spirit, you are not a true son or daughter. Remember that the Spirit and the Word must agree. God will not go against His Word. Any leading that is against the Word of God is therefore not of the Spirit. True sons and daughters follow the Holy Spirit's lead.

Again, I strongly believe that a major move of God is now upon the earth. The true end-time sons and daughters of God are going to be shown forth in the earth with the demonstrative power and Word of God!

PROPHETIC INTEL

The Bible reveals that in this time period, your own sons and daughters (even to your grandchildren and beyond) will prophesy. To prophesy is to foretell. It is to, by way of the Holy Spirit, predict the future. It's time for you to embrace and activate your children in the prophetic.

My mother, Debra Giles, has been a powerful prayer warrior, intercessor, and minister. She has been in ministry for nearly forty years. The Lord used her to help train me in the prophetic, and to give me an understanding that I was a prophet due to the visitations, dreams, and visions I would have as a child. She has written a book I want to recommend, *Raising Prophetic*

Kids (Chosen, 2024), that goes into great detail about how to nurture your children and grandchildren to walk in their prophetic purpose.

I also want to lead you in doing the following simple activation exercise with your children. Or if you are a young person, do this yourself. In fact, anyone of any age can benefit from doing this exercise. You don't have to be a parent or child to practice with it; you simply have to want to grow in the prophetic.

1. Take five minutes to pray and ask the Lord to use you as a vessel to encourage or uplift someone else. (If you're doing this activation with your children, then pray along with them.) Ask God whom He wants you to give a message to.

2. After you pray, sit quietly and wait for a person to come to mind. You may see his or her face as a mental picture, or you may hear the person's name. Or you may just sense that a particular person keeps coming to your mind.

3. Pray again for a couple of minutes, this time with a pen and paper close by. Ask God if there is an encouraging word that He desires to speak to the person. You or your child write down what you hear, perceive, or feel in your spirit from the Lord.

4. Take faith and reach out to that person to share what you believe God has shared with you. It's okay to say to him or her, "I believe [or I think] God has shared this message with me for you . . ."

This simple exercise will help build the faith of you and your children to prophesy and speak the words of the Lord, because when God speaks, He may speak through you!

Conclusion

Intelligence Mission

This book has been an adventure and a journey for me to write. I went through such intense and extreme warfare to write it. I experienced tremendous warfare against my body, my family, and my ministry. But the Lord gave us all powerful testimonies where we prevailed. I'm only sharing this to bring glory to God and to show that the enemy did not want this information and revelation in your hands. Revelation 19:10 says that "the testimony of Jesus is the spirit of prophecy." That's right—He is the spirit of prophecy. When we speak His words, we testify of Him. This is the reason why pure, biblical, and sound prophetic ministry is so valuable today.

This book is composed of three parts meant to help you fully understand and digest the information I've presented about when God speaks. Now that you have read it, I want to make sure that you got the most from the information. Let me summarize briefly what we covered. The first part of the book was "Understanding Your Prophetic Nature." God wants to partner with you to see His plans come to pass in the earth. Isn't that an amazing thing? The Ancient of Days created you brilliantly. He loves you so much and wants to collaborate with you to effect positive change in the world. That's humbling even to think of. You, too, can prophesy; you, too, can hear from God. Although those who operate in the office of a prophet, as well as the other five-fold ministers, are needed, you don't have to be dependent on a single other person in order to connect to and hear from God personally. Jesus Christ wants a deeply personal and real relationship with you. When you accept Him into your heart and surrender to Him, you will discover that He has placed His word in you. You carry the future. You can speak those things forth that have not yet occurred. What a beautiful thing!

In the second part of the book, "A Glimpse into the Future," we got down to the meat of the content. The prophetic words, biblical teachings, practical stories, and insights I included in this second part were written to help admonish you, warn you, encourage you, prepare you, and uplift you. I hope you will use this part as a reference to go back to again and again. When you see the prophecies coming to pass and featured in the headline news, look back at them as a reference and a reminder that God does speak today. Also reread the words to see if there were instructions on what to do when those things occur, or if they signaled something else coming behind them. Lastly, take those prophetic words into prayer with you and listen for the Lord to speak to you about them. If you have a relationship with the Father, He will show you how to apply the information you've read here in your personal life.

The third part of the book was called "God's Kingdom Advancing." I spoke in this final section about the triumphant rise and progression of the Church of the Lord Jesus Christ. That means you will have a triumphant rise because you are the Church. You are called out and set apart for His use. I hope the chapters you read in that final section have lit a fire for you to draw close to your first love. I hope the words have pushed you to know Him more.

Now that you've read this book, you have a mission. Prophetic intelligence doesn't stop when you've finished reading. Your prophetic intelligence mission is just beginning. You can hear when God speaks, and you have a responsibility to carry the heart, message, and word of Jesus Christ wherever you go. You are a prophetic sign and wonder. You are a word and answer to someone's prayer.

There will be much darkness in our world, and it will escalate as the days, months, and years progress. Yet you have learned how to thrive in uncertain times and have gained confidence for your future. Now you must be the light in the darkness so that others can do the same. You must be the salt of the earth. You must be a city on a hill, put there to demonstrate the power of God. You have a mission to be the testimony of Jesus Christ. So prophesy when God speaks, and watch things change around you for the better!

Notes

Chapter 1 You Carry the Future

1. Blue Letter Bible, "ôwlâm" (Strong's H5769), accessed August 20, 2024, https://www
.blueletterbible.org/lexicon/h5769/nasb20/wlc/0-1/.

2. *Dictionary.com*, "activate," accessed August 20, 2024, https://www.dictionary.com
/browse/activate.

Chapter 2 God Still Speaks Today

1. Blue Letter Bible, "yāḏa" (Strong's H3045), accessed August 20, 2024, https://www
.blueletterbible.org/lexicon/h3045/hnv/wlc/0-1/.

2. Bible Study Tools, "gnosis" (Strong's G1108), accessed August 20, 2024, https://www
.biblestudytools.com/lexicons/greek/kjv/gnosis.html.

3. *Dictionary.com*, "invention," accessed August 20, 2024, https://www.dictionary.com
/browse/invention.

Chapter 3 It Might Sound Crazy, but I'm Hearing God

1. Margaret Rouse, "Radio Frequency," Technopedia, last updated October 16, 2023,
https://www.techopedia.com/definition/5083/radio-frequency-rf.

2. *Britannica*, "frequency (physics)," accessed August 20, 2024, https://www.britannica
.com/science/frequency-physics.

3. Bible Study Tools, "gabahh" (Strong's H1361), accessed August 20, 2024, https://www
.biblestudytools.com/lexicons/hebrew/kjv/gabahh.html.

4. Bible Study Tools, "chazown" (Strong's H2377), accessed August 20, 2024, https://
www.biblestudytools.com/lexicons/hebrew/kjv/chazown.html.

5. Allen G. Schick, Lawrence A. Gordon, and Susan Haka, "Information overload: A
temporal approach," *Accounting, Organizations and Society* 15, no. 3 (1990), 199–220; see
full article at https://www.sciencedirect.com/science/article/abs/pii/036136829090005F.

Chapter 4 God Speaks through Numb3rs

1. Note that throughout this chapter, the meanings of various Hebrew letters and words,
and also Latin words, come from the previous research I've done on the Hebrew alphabet

and on this topic of God speaking through numbers. One of the main sources I drew from was the Hebrew for Christians website, particularly the Grammar section's "Unit One: The Alphabet." See https://www.hebrew4christians.com/Grammar/Unit_One/unit_one.html. I also drew from Chabad.org, particularly the Learning & Values section's "Essentials: Hebrew: Letters of Light." See https://www.chabad.org/library/article_cdo/aid/137068/jewish/Letters-of-Light.htm.

Chapter 5 Alternate Timeline

1. For more information about the LHC, visit https://home.cern/science/accelerators/large-hadron-collider.
2. For more on dark matter, visit Robert Lea, "What is dark energy?", SPACE.com, November 24, 2022, https://www.space.com/dark-energy-what-is-it.
3. For more on this, see https://home.cern/science/computing/birth-web.
4. For more on this, see https://home.cern/science/physics/higgs-boson.
5. Bible Study Tools, "chamac" (Strong's H2554), accessed August 20, 2024, https://www.biblestudytools.com/lexicons/hebrew/kjv/chamac.html.

Chapter 7 Genetic Recoding

1. Bible Study Tools, "nphiyl" (Strong's H5303), accessed August 20, 2024, https://www.biblestudytools.com/lexicons/hebrew/kjv/nephiyl.html.
2. Bible Study Tools, "doxa" (Strong's G1391), accessed August 20, 2024, https://www.biblestudytools.com/lexicons/greek/kjv/doxa.html.
3. Bible Study Tools "`Anaq" (Strong's H6061), accessed August 20, 2024, https://www.biblestudytools.com/lexicons/hebrew/kjv/anaq-4.html.

Chapter 8 Superstorms

1. *Oxford Reference*, "element" (Overview), accessed August 20, 2024, https://www.oxfordreference.com/display/10.1093/oi/authority.20110803095746742.
2. *Dictionary.com*, "govern," accessed August 20, 2024, https://www.dictionary.com/browse/govern.
3. *Dictionary.com*, "dominion," accessed August 20, 2024, https://www.dictionary.com/browse/dominion.
4. Bible Study Tools, "Tsavah" (Strong's H6680), accessed August 20, 2024, https://www.biblestudytools.com/lexicons/hebrew/kjv/tsavah.html.
5. See again this chapter's note 1. See also *Merriam-Webster Dictionary*, "element," accessed August 20, 2024, https://www.merriam-webster.com/dictionary/elements.
6. *Dictionary.com*, "earth," accessed August 20, 2024, https://www.dictionary.com/browse/earth.
7. *Latdict*, "terra, terrae," accessed August 20, 2024, https://latin-dictionary.net/definition/37005/terra-terrae.
8. Bible Study Tools, "radah" (Strong's H7287), accessed August 20, 2024, https://www.biblestudytools.com/lexicons/hebrew/kjv/radah.html.
9. Bible Study Tools, "nepios" (Strong's G3516), accessed August 20, 2024, https://www.biblestudytools.com/lexicons/greek/nas/nepios.html.
10. Bible Study Tools, "anemos" (Strong's G417), accessed August 20, 2024, https://www.biblestudytools.com/lexicons/greek/kjv/anemos.html.

11. *Oxford Reference*, "wind," accessed August 20, 2024, https://www.oxfordreference .com/display/10.1093/acref/9780198609810.001.0001/acref-9780198609810-e-7723.
12. Numerous online sites give this same definition for the word *tornado*.

Chapter 11 AI and the Beast System

1. For more details about John's exile on the island of Patmos, see Margaret Hunter, "John Exiled to Patmos," Amazing Bible Timeline, February 22, 2013, https://amazingbible timeline.com/blog/john-exiled-to-patmos/.

Chapter 12 Blackout

1. Statista Research Department, "Number of satellites in orbit by major country as of April 20, 2022," statista.com, May 24, 2024, https://www.statista.com/statistics/264472 /number-of-satellites-in-orbit-by-operating-country/.
2. Bible Study Tools, "qowl" (Strong's H6963), accessed August 20, 2024, https://www .biblestudytools.com/lexicons/hebrew/kjv/qowl.html.
3. Blue Letter Bible, "ḥāṣaṣ" (Strong's H2686), accessed August 20, 2024, https://www .blueletterbible.org/lexicon/h2686/web/wlc/0-1/.
4. Bible Study Tools, "radah" (Strong's H7287), accessed August 20, 2024, https://www .biblestudytools.com/lexicons/hebrew/kjv/radah.html.

Chapter 13 Clash of Crowns

1. Oxford English Dictionary, "Terrorism," accessed August 20, 2024, https://www.oed .com/search/dictionary/?scope=Entries&q=terrorism.

Chapter 14 Inventions and Medical Advances

1. Bible Study Tools, "machashabah" (Strong's H4284), accessed August 20, 2024, https:// www.biblestudytools.com/lexicons/hebrew/kjv/machashabah.html.
2. Bible Study Tools, "zamam" (Strong's H2161), accessed August 20, 2024, https://www .biblestudytools.com/lexicons/hebrew/kjv/zamam.html.
3. Bible Study Tools, "pharmakeia" (Strong's G5331), accessed August 20, 2024, https:// www.biblestudytools.com/lexicons/greek/kjv/pharmakeia.html.
4. Statista Research Department, "Market Insights > Health: Global pharmaceutical industry—statistics & facts," statista.com, https://www.statista.com/outlook/hmo/phar maceuticals/worldwide.

Chapter 15 Back to Acts

1. *ESV Study Bible* (Wheaton, Ill.: Crossway/Good News Publishers, 2007), 1811.
2. For more on this, see C. Marvin Pate et al., *The Story of Israel: A Biblical Theology* (Downers Grove, Ill.: InterVarsity Press, 2004), 88.
3. *ESV Study Bible*, 2075.
4. Bible Study Tools, "chayah" (Strong's H2421), accessed August 20, 2024, https://www .biblestudytools.com/lexicons/hebrew/kjv/chayah.html.
5. Owen Jarus and Jessie Szalay, "The Renaissance: The 'Rebirth' of science & culture," LiveScience, January 11, 2022, https://www.livescience.com/55230-renaissance.html.

Chapter 16 The Remnant Church Rising

1. *Merriam-Webster Dictionary*, "travail," accessed August 20, 2024, https://www.mer riam-webster.com/dictionary/travail.

2. Bible Study Tools, "gnosis" (Strong's G1108), accessed August 20, 2024, https://www .biblestudytools.com/lexicons/greek/kjv/gnosis.html.

3. Bible Study Tools, "diakrisis" (Strong's G1253), accessed August 20, 2024, https:// www.biblestudytools.com/lexicons/greek/nas/diakrisis.html.

Chapter 17 A Prophetic Generation

1. *Dictionary.com*, "barbarous," accessed August 20, 2024, https://www.dictionary.com /browse/barbarous.

2. Ibid.

3. *Oxford Reference*, "passion," accessed August 20, 2024, https://www.oxfordreference .com/display/10.1093/acref/9780190681166.001.0001/acref-9780190681166-e-237.

4. *Merriam-Webster Dictionary*, "suffer," accessed August 20, 2024, https://www.merr iam-webster.com/dictionary/suffer.

5. Bible Study Tools, "hupomeno" (Strong's G5278), accessed August 20, 2024, https:// www.biblestudytools.com/lexicons/greek/kjv/hupomeno.html.

6. Ibid.

7. *Dictionary.com*, "abide," accessed August 20, 2024, https://www.dictionary.com /browse/abide.

8. Ibid. See also Bible Study Tools, "meno" (Strong's G3306), accessed August 20, 2024, https://www.biblestudytools.com/lexicons/greek/kjv/meno.html.

9. *Dictionary.com*, "persist" (see under the "Word History and Origins" heading), accessed August 20, 2024, https://www.dictionary.com/browse/persist.

10. *Dictionary.com*, "press," accessed August 20, 2024, https://www.dictionary.com /browse/press.

11. *Dictionary.com*, "forward," accessed August 20, 2024, https://www.dictionary.com /browse/forward.

12. Bible Study Tools, "Shem" (Strong's H8035), accessed August 20, 2024, https://www .biblestudytools.com/lexicons/hebrew/kjv/shem-2.html.

JOSHUA GILES is an apostle, prophet, bestselling author, and sought-after conference speaker. He is the lead pastor and founder of Kingdom Embassy Worship Center in Minneapolis, Minnesota, and founder of Joshua Giles Ministries and the Mantle Network. Joshua reaches out internationally through apostolic centers, prophetic schools, and training modules. He has traveled to more than 35 nations to minister the Gospel, and to advise government officials, dignitaries, and national leaders seeking prophetic counsel.

Further, Joshua is an anointed media influencer whose popular podcast shows have garnered over a quarter of a million downloads. His online prophetic forecast live stream has over 110,000 subscribers. He has also been featured on numerous national and international television and media outlets.

Joshua has a double bachelor's degree in business management and psychology, and a master's degree in theological studies. He devotes his time to helping Christian entrepreneurs, training leaders, and empowering believers. He has a great desire to help others succeed in what God has called them to do. More than anything, it is his ultimate desire to do the will of God for his life.

Connect with Joshua

JOSHUAGILES.COM

@ProphetJoshuaGiles

@JoshuaGilesGlobal

@JoshuaGilesMinistries